NEW 2018

by ARGO BROTHERS

COMMON CORE MATH

GRADE 6

PART I: MULTIPLE CHOICE

Visit **www.argoprep.com** to get
FREE access to our online platform.

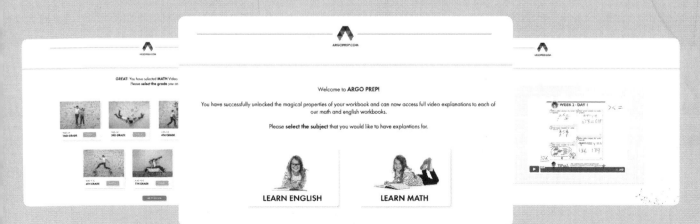

1000+ Minutes of Video Explanations and more!

Authors: Kellie Zimmer
                      Anayet Chowdhury
                      Eduard Suleyman
                      Vladislav Suleyman

Design: Vladislav Suleyman

At Argo Brothers, we are dedicated to providing quality and effective supplemental practice for your child. We would love to hear your honest feedback and **review** of our workbooks on **Amazon**.

Argo Brothers is one of the leading providers of supplemental educational products and services. We offer affordable and effective test prep solutions to educators, parents and students. Learning should be fun and easy! For that reason, most of our workbooks come with detailed video answer explanations taught by one of our fabulous instructors. Our goal is to make your life easier, so let us know how we can help you by e-mailing us at **info@argobrothers.com**.

ARGO BROTHERS

OTHER BOOKS BY ARGO BROTHERS

Here are some other test prep workbooks by Argo Brothers you may be interested in. All of our workbooks come equipped with detailed video explanations to make your learning experience a breeze! Subscribe to our mailing list at www.argobrothers.com to receive custom updates about your education.

GRADE 2

GRADE 3

GRADE 4

GRADE 5

GRADE 6

GRADE 7

GRADE 4

GRADE 5

TABLE OF CONTENTS

Week 1 7

Week 2 13

Week 3 19

Week 4 25

Week 5 31

Week 6 37

Week 7 43

Week 8 49

Week 9 55

Week 10 61

Week 11 67

Week 12 73

Week 13 79

Week 14 85

Week 15 91

Week 16 97

Week 17 103

Week 18 109

Week 19 115

Week 20 121

End of Year Assessment 128

Answer Keys. 138

HOW TO USE
THE BOOK

This workbook is designed to give lots of practice with the math Common Core State Standards (CCSS). By practicing and mastering this entire workbook, your child will become very familiar and comfortable with the state math exam. If you are a teacher using this workbook for your student's, you will notice each question is labeled with the specific standard so you can easily assign your students problems in the workbook. This workbook takes the CCSS and divides them up among 20 weeks. By working on these problems on a daily basis, students will be able to (1) find any deficiencies in their understanding and/or practice of math and (2) have small successes each day that will build proficiency and confidence in their abilities.

You can find detailed video explanations to each problem in the book by visiting:
www.argoprep.com

We strongly recommend watching the videos as it will reinforce the fundamental concepts. Please note, scrap paper may be necessary while using this workbook so that the student has sufficient space to show their work.

For a detailed overview of the Common Core State Standards for 6th grade, please visit:
www.corestandards.org/Math/Content/6/introduction/

For more practice with 6th Grade Math, be sure to check out our other book, Common Core Math Workbook Grade 6: Free Response

WEEK 1

You want to become better at math and that process will start now. This week you will practice dividing with fractions, solving word problems and using models to represent problems.

You can find detailed video explanations to each problem in the book by visiting:
ArgoPrep.com

1. The length of a cell is 2/3 mm. If the area of the cell is 1/12 square mm, what is the width of the cell?

A. $\frac{1}{2}$ mm   C. $\frac{1}{6}$ mm

B. $\frac{1}{3}$ mm   D. $\frac{1}{8}$ mm

6.NS.1

2. How many cups of yogurt would 5 people get if they equally shared 3/4 cup of yogurt?

A. $\frac{3}{20}$ cup   C. $\frac{5}{4}$ cup

B. $\frac{3}{5}$ cup   D. $\frac{5}{3}$ cup

6.NS.1

3. The area of a rectangular skate park is 6/11 square miles. The length of the park is 3/5 mile. What is the width, in miles, of the park?

A. $\frac{18}{55}$ mile   C. $\frac{11}{10}$ miles

B. $\frac{10}{11}$ mile   D. $\frac{55}{18}$ miles

6.NS.1

4. Which expression is modeled by the diagram below?

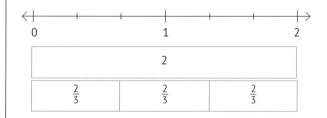

A. $\frac{1}{3} \div 2$

B. $2 \div \frac{1}{3}$

C. $\frac{2}{3} \div 2$

D. $2 \div \frac{2}{3}$

6.NS.1

5. How wide is a rectangular strip of land with length 7/8 mile and area 7/16 square miles?

A. $\frac{1}{2}$ mile   C. $\frac{1}{8}$ mile

B. $\frac{1}{4}$ mile   D. $\frac{1}{16}$ mile

6.NS.1

6. How many ½-cup servings are in 3½ cups of soup?

A. 2   C. 5

B. 3   D. 7

6.NS.1

To find the area of a space, you multiply the length times the width.

1. The area of a rectangular parking lot is 8/45 square kilometers. The length of the lot is 4/9 kilometer. What is the width, in km, of the parking lot?

A. $\frac{4}{45}$ km

C. $\frac{8}{9}$ km

B. $\frac{2}{5}$ km

D. $2\frac{1}{4}$ km

6.NS.1

2. The length of a rectangular placemat is 2/3 foot. If the area of the placemat is 1/2 square foot, what is the width of the placemat?

A. $\frac{1}{3}$ foot

C. $\frac{3}{4}$ foot

B. $\frac{1}{4}$ foot

D. $\frac{4}{3}$ foot

6.NS.1

3. Which expression is modeled by the diagram below?

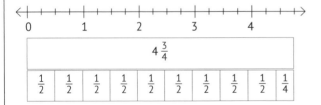

A. $4\frac{3}{4} \div \frac{1}{2}$

C. $\frac{1}{2} \div 4\frac{3}{4}$

B. $4 \div \frac{3}{4}$

D. $\frac{3}{4} \div 4$

6.NS.1

4. What is the value of $\frac{8}{9} \div \frac{5}{12}$?

A. $\frac{5}{12}$

C. $\frac{10}{27}$

B. $\frac{8}{15}$

D. $2\frac{2}{15}$

6.NS.1

5. The length of a card is 1/3-cm. If the area of the card is 4/15 square cm, what is the width of the card?

A. $\frac{1}{5}$ cm

D. $\frac{4}{5}$ cm

B. $\frac{2}{3}$ cm

C. $\frac{3}{4}$ cm

6.NS.1

6. How many cups of pudding would 4 people get if they equally shared 3¼ cup of pudding?

A. $\frac{13}{16}$ cups

B. $\frac{16}{13}$ cups

C. 13 cups

D. 16 cups

6.NS.1

If you have the area and need the length, you divide the area by the width and the quotient is the length.

9

1. Which expression is modeled by the diagram below?

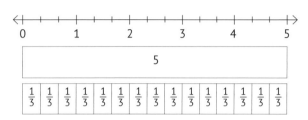

A. $5 \div \frac{1}{3}$

C. $5 \times \frac{1}{3}$

B. $\frac{1}{3} \div 5$

D. $\frac{1}{3} \times 5$

6.NS.1

2. The carpet remnant was 4 1/8 square units. If the remnant was 3/4 units wide, what was its length?

A. $3 \frac{3}{8}$ units

C. $8 \frac{1}{4}$ units

B. $5 \frac{1}{2}$ units

D. $11 \frac{1}{2}$ units

6.NS.1

3. There are 4 friends who want to share $10 \frac{2}{3}$ gallons of tea. How many gallons will each friend get?

A. $2 \frac{1}{2}$

C. $3 \frac{1}{3}$

B. $2 \frac{2}{3}$

D. $3 \frac{3}{4}$

6.NS.1

4. How many $\frac{1}{4}$ - cup servings are in $7 \frac{1}{2}$ cups of espresso?

A. 15

B. 21

C. 28

D. 30

6.NS.1

5. The length of a photograph is 1 4/5 inches. If the area of the photo is 33/20 square inches, what is the width of the photograph?

A. $\frac{20}{33}$ inch

C. $\frac{3}{4}$ inches

B. $\frac{11}{12}$ inch

D. $\frac{4}{3}$ inches

6.NS.1

6. How many fifths are in $\frac{4}{10}$?

A. $\frac{1}{2}$

D. 2

B. 1

C. $1 \frac{1}{2}$

6.NS.1

There are 4 fourths in one whole.

1. There are $10\frac{1}{2}$ cookies. If Aaron and Bentley share them equally, how many cookies will each boy receive?

A. $4\frac{3}{4}$ **C.** $6\frac{1}{2}$

B. $5\frac{1}{4}$ **D.** $8\frac{1}{2}$

6.NS.1

2. How many $\frac{1}{6}$-liter servings are in $4\frac{2}{3}$ liters?

A. 25
B. 26
C. 27
D. 28

6.NS.1

3. The napkin was 3 1/4 inches wide and had an area of 16 1/4 square inches. What is the length of the napkin?

A. 4 inches
B. 5 inches
C. 6 inches
D. 7 inches

6.NS.1

4. Which expression is modeled by the diagram below?

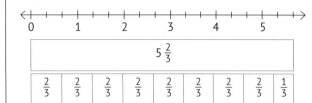

A. $5\frac{2}{3} \div \frac{2}{3}$ **C.** $5 \div \frac{1}{3}$

B. $\frac{2}{3} \div 5\frac{2}{3}$ **D.** $5 \div \frac{2}{3}$

6.NS.1

5. How many $\frac{1}{12}$-gallon servings are in 12 gallons?

A. 1
B. 24
C. 144
D. 288

6.NS.1

6. The floor was 8 3/4 yards wide and had an area of 78 3/4 square yards. What is the length of the floor?

A. 7 yards
B. 8 yards
C. 9 yards
D. 10 yards

6.NS.1

When people are sharing, make sure to find the correct number of people first before making any math calculations.

11

1. How many fourths are in $7\frac{6}{8}$?

    A. 13

    B. 31

    C. 56

    D. 62

6.NS.1

2. How many $\frac{1}{3}$ - cup servings are in $3\frac{1}{2}$ cups of chai?

    A. $9\frac{1}{2}$ **C.** $10\frac{1}{2}$

    B. 10   **D.** 11

6.NS.1

3. The length of a computer case is 12 1/2 inches. If the area of the case is 103 1/8 square inches, what is the width of the computer case?

    A. $7\frac{3}{4}$ inches   **D.** $9\frac{3}{4}$ inches

    B. $8\frac{1}{4}$ inches

    C. $9\frac{1}{2}$ inches

6.NS.1

4. A race is to be $20\frac{4}{5}$ kilometers long and each runner is to run $\frac{1}{4}$ of the race. How far will each runner run?

    A. $5\frac{1}{5}$ km   **C.** $6\frac{2}{5}$ km

    B. $5\frac{4}{5}$ km   **D.** $7\frac{1}{5}$ km

6.NS.1

5. The area of the dance classroom was 418 square meters. If the width is $16\frac{1}{2}$ meters, what is the length, in meters, of the dance room?

    A. $2\frac{1}{6}$ meters   **C.** $25\frac{1}{3}$ meters

    B. $8\frac{5}{6}$ meters   **D.** $26\frac{1}{8}$ meters

6.NS.1

6. Which expression is modeled by the diagram below?

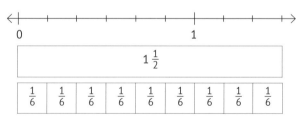

    A. $\frac{1}{6} \div 1\frac{1}{2}$ **C.** $1 \div \frac{1}{6}$

    B. $1\frac{1}{6} \div \frac{1}{1}$ **D.** $1\frac{1}{2} \div \frac{1}{6}$

6.NS.1

DAY 6
CHALLENGE QUESTION

If there are 15 one-quarter cup servings of ice cream in a container, how many cups does the container hold? 6.NS.1

12

In Week 2 you will get lots of practice dividing multi-digit numbers as well as adding, subtracting, multiplying and dividing decimal numbers.

You can find detailed video explanations to each problem in the book by visiting:
ArgoPrep.com

1. What is the quotient of 1365 and 13?

A. 15
B. 105
C. 150
D. 155

6.NS.2

2. What is 2408 ÷ 20?

A. 120 r 8
B. 125 r 12
C. 200 r 16
D. 1200 r 0

6.NS.2

3. Arthur had 986 vests that he had to ship. He could only put 15 vests in a box. How many FULL boxes would Arthur have?

A. 61
B. 63
C. 65
D. 66

6.NS.2

4. Annie baked 219 cookies for the bake sale. Each bag can contain 4 cookies. How many bags would she need if she bagged ALL of the cookies?

A. 52
B. 53
C. 54
D. 55

6.NS.2

5. Allyson split her 154 quarters up evenly among her 7 friends. How many quarters did Allyson give each friend?

A. 20
B. 22
C. 24
D. 26

6.NS.2

6. How many $\frac{1}{10}$ - liter servings are in $7\frac{2}{5}$ liters of punch?

A. $7\frac{3}{10}$
C. 73

B. $7\frac{4}{5}$
D. 74

6.NS.1

When dividing, if the divisor does not go into a number at least once, please make sure to use a zero to hold the place.

1. What is 9,009 ÷ 33?

- **A.** 273
- **B.** 283
- **C.** 293
- **D.** 303

6.NS.2

2. What is the quotient of 6,559 and 21?

- **A.** 312
- **B.** 312 r 3
- **C.** 312 r 7
- **D.** 312 r 15

6.NS.2

3. The tree trunk was 186 feet tall. If each piece of trunk was cut so that it was 9 feet long, how many 9-foot pieces could be made from the tree's trunk?

- **A.** 20
- **B.** 168
- **C.** 200
- **D.** 1,674

6.NS.2

4. There were 657 desks that needed to be placed evenly into 25 classrooms. What is the smallest number of desks each class would have?

- **A.** 23
- **B.** 26
- **C.** 29
- **D.** 32

6.NS.2

5. There were 1549 cars that were be to be parked on 17 lots. If each lot received the exact same number of cars, how many cars would NOT be able to be placed on a lot?

- **A.** 2
- **B.** 7
- **C.** 11
- **D.** 14

6.NS.2

6. The length of Asa's suitcase is 19 3/4 inches. If the area of the case is 266 5/8 square inches, what is the width of the Asa's suitcase?

- **A.** $12\frac{1}{3}$ inches
- **C.** 13 inches
- **B.** $12\frac{3}{4}$ inches
- **D.** $13\frac{1}{2}$ inches

6.NS.1

When reading a word problem, if it says that something will be shared evenly, that indicates there is division involved.

1. Allen had 12 goals on the season. If he played in 8 games, how many goals did he average per game? Round your answer to the nearest hundredth.

A. 0.67
B. 1.5
C. 2.3
D. 3.2

6.NS.3

2. The first worm was 12.8 cm long. The second worm was 1.6 times as long as the first worm. How long was the second worm?

A. 8 cm
B. 11.2 cm
C. 14.4 cm
D. 20.48 cm

6.NS.3

3. Arial was saving money for a new bike. She had $78 in her account when she received $98.57 for her birthday. She then spent $12.48 on some music. How much money does Arial have available for her bike?

A. $33.05
B. $164.09
C. $176.57
D. $189.05

6.NS.3

4. Andrea had 12 yards of ribbon and each bow required 2.6 yards. How many complete bows can Andrea make with her ribbon?

A. 4
B. 5
C. 6
D. 7

6.NS.3

5. What is the solution of the equation below?

$y - 3.8 = 12.4$

A. $y = -8.6$
B. $y = 3.3$
C. $y = 8.6$
D. $y = 16.2$

6.NS.3

6. Alex went on a trip that was 8,216 miles long. If he drove the same distance each day and the trip took him 13 days, how far did Alex drive each day?

A. 632 miles
B. 638 miles
C. 642 miles
D. 646 miles

6.NS.2

When dividing by a decimal number, remember that you move the decimal point as many places as necessary to obtain a whole number. (You also must move the decimal point the same number of places in the dividend as well.)

1. There are 12 kittens. If they all average 4.7 pounds, what is the total weight of all 12 kittens?

   A. 2.6 pounds
   B. 16.7 pounds
   C. 36.5 pounds
   D. 56.4 pounds

   6.NS.3

3. How much farther did Angelica walk than Catie?

   A. 1.1 km
   B. 2.7 km
   C. 3.1 km
   D. 4.2 km

   6.NS.3

2. The 6 children had 35.4 pounds of candy to share. How many pounds of candy would each child get?

   A. 5.8 pounds
   B. 5.9 pounds
   C. 6.0 pounds
   D. 6.1 pounds

   6.NS.3

4. How much farther did Dixon walk than Brent?

   A. 1.1 km
   B. 2.7 km
   C. 3.1 km
   D. 4.2 km

   6.NS.3

The chart below shows the distance that 4 students walked on Saturday. **Use the information to answer questions 3 – 5.**

Student	Distance (km)
Angelica	12.6
Brent	8.4
Catie	9.9
Dixon	11.5

5. What is the total distance the 4 students walked?

   A. 32.4 km
   B. 37.4 km
   C. 42.4 km
   D. 45.4 km

   6.NS.3

When answering word problems, check for key words that can tell you whether to use addition, subtraction, multiplication and/or division.

WEEK 2 · DAY 5

ASSESSMENT

1. The length of a tarp is 4 1/5 meters. If the area of the tarp is 27 3/10 square meters, what is the width of the tarp?

A. $5\frac{1}{15}$ meters   **C.** $6\frac{1}{3}$ meters

B. $5\frac{4}{5}$ meters   **D.** $6\frac{1}{2}$ meters

6.NS.1

2. Bella packed 12 cupcakes in each box. If she had 400 cupcakes to package, how many full boxes would she have?

A. 31
B. 32
C. 33
D. 34

6.NS.2

3. What is 7,511 ÷ 37?

A. 23
B. 203
C. 230
D. 233

6.NS.2

4. Bruce had 36.5 feet of twine to tie up some packages. He used 4.3 feet on 3 packages and 8.1 on another package. How much twine did Bruce have left?

A. 15.5 feet
B. 21.1 feet
C. 24.1 feet
D. 28.4 feet

6.NS.3

5. Benny used 4.6 pounds of butter for his pound cake. Alicia uses 2.1 times that amount. How much butter does Alicia use? Round your answer to the nearest tenth.

A. 2.2 pounds
B. 2.5 pounds
C. 6.7 pounds
D. 9.7 pounds

6.NS.3

6. Last month the donut shop made 6.270 donuts. If there were 30 days last month and they made the same number of donuts each day, how many donuts were made each day?

A. 29
B. 209
C. 290
D. 299

6.NS.3

DAY 6

CHALLENGE QUESTION

Carson was 20.8 inches tall. His dad was 3.1 times that height and his uncle was 5 ½ inches shorter than Carson's dad. How tall was Carson's uncle? Round your answer to the nearest inch.

6.NS.3

WEEK 3

VIDEO EXPLANATIONS

ARGOPREP.COM

Week 3 is fun! You can find the GCF (greatest common factor) and LCM (least common multiple) among 2 or 3 numbers. You will also begin using positive and negative numbers, which are helpful in real life – banking, hiking, temperatures and more!

You can find detailed video explanations to each problem in the book by visiting:
ArgoPrep.com

1. What is the greatest common factor of 36 and 48?

A. 3
B. 4
C. 9
D. 12

6.NS.4

2. What is the least common multiple of 9 and 6?

A. 3
B. 12
C. 18
D. 54

6.NS.4

3. Bryson can run a lap in 5 minutes and Anabeth can run a lap in 6 minutes. If they start running at the same time and place on the track, how many minutes will it be before they are both at the starting point?

A. 1 minute
B. 11 minutes
C. 15 minutes
D. 30 minutes

6.NS.4

Below is a schedule of how often 3 subway lines can complete their routes. All routes start at The Center stop. **Use the information to answer questions 4 – 5.**

Line	Route Time
Express	12 minutes
Standard	15 minutes
Local	8 minutes

4. If the Local and Express lines leave The Center at the same time and run continuously, how long before they would <u>both</u> leave The Center again?

A. 4 minutes
B. 16 minutes
C. 20 minutes
D. 24 minutes

6.NS.4

5. If the Standard and Express lines leave The Center at the same time and run continuously, how long before they would <u>both</u> leave The Center again?

A. 24 minutes
B. 45 minutes
C. 60 minutes
D. 90 minutes

6.NS.4

The GCF is the Greatest Common Factor and it is the largest number two of its multiples have in common.

1. The trip from Denver to Chicago and back takes 12 days by train and 8 days by bus. If the trips are run consecutively, how many days will it be before the train and bus leave Denver at the same time?

- **A.** 4 days
- **B.** 16 days
- **C.** 24 days
- **D.** 96 days

6.NS.4

2. What is the greatest common factor of 43 and 47?

- **A.** 1
- **B.** 3
- **C.** 7
- **D.** 13

6.NS.4

3. How many $\frac{1}{4}$ - cup servings are in $\frac{7}{8}$ cups of ice cream?

- **A.** $\frac{2}{7}$
- **C.** $3\frac{1}{2}$
- **B.** $\frac{7}{32}$
- **D.** $4\frac{4}{7}$

6.NS.1

4. What is the greatest common factor of 38 and 76?

- **A.** 2
- **B.** 19
- **C.** 38
- **D.** 76

6.NS.4

5. What is the least common multiple of 12 and 8?

- **A.** 4
- **B.** 8
- **C.** 16
- **D.** 24

6.NS.4

6. Each grocery bag contains 1 package of flour and 2 packages of sugar. If a package of flour weighs 3.1 kilograms and a package of sugar weighs 4.8 kilograms, what is the combined weight of 2 grocery bags?

- **A.** 12.7 kg
- **B.** 15.8 kg
- **C.** 25.4 kg
- **D.** 31.6 kg

6.NS.3

The LCM stands for Least Common Multiple and is the smallest number that 2 (or more) factors both have.

1. Bennett had a negative balance of -$51.47 at the beginning of the day. By the end of the day his balance was zero. Which statement best describes what happened?

   A. Bennett withdrew $51.47.
   B. Bennett deposited $51.47.
   C. Bennett borrowed $51.47.
   D. Bennett spent $51.47.

   6.NS.5

2. Barron had $879 of debt. Which action will allow Barron to become debt-free?

   A. Barron can borrow $879 from his parents to pay off his loan.
   B. Barron can pay $789 on his loan.
   C. Barron can spend $879.
   D. Barron can pay $879 on his loan.

   6.NS.5

3. The rain gauge measures 4.7 centimeters. How would the water level need to change so that the gauge measures 0 centimeters?

   A. −2.35 cm
   B. +2.35 cm
   C. −4.7 cm
   D. +4.7 cm

   6.NS.5

4. What is the least common multiple of 11 and 3?

   A. 14
   B. 33
   C. 43
   D. 66

   6.NS.4

5. What is the greatest common factor of 51 and 99?

   A. 1
   B. 3
   C. 11
   D. 17

   6.NS.4

6. The length of a tablecloth is 8 1/3 feet. If the area of the tablecloth is 40 square feet, what is the width of the tablecloth?

   A. $4\frac{1}{3}$ feet   **D.** $5\frac{2}{5}$ feet

   B. $4\frac{4}{5}$ feet

   C. $5\frac{1}{4}$ feet

   6.NS.1

When opposite numbers are added together, the result is 0.

1. The temperature is –2.1°C. How would the temperature need to change so that the temperature is 0°C?

- **A.** –2.1°C
- **B.** +2.1°C
- **C.** –1.2°C
- **D.** +1.2°C

6.NS.5

2. Billy is at 720 feet above sea level. How many feet should he travel to reach sea level?

- **A.** – 360 feet
- **B.** 360 feet
- **C.** – 720 feet
- **D.** 720 feet

6.NS.5

3. Which expression is equivalent to:

5 (8 + 3)?

- **A.** 58 + 53
- **B.** 58 + 3
- **C.** 40 + 15
- **D.** 40 + 3

6.NS.4

4. What is the value of t in the equation below?

$14.8 - t = 0$

- **A.** $t = 7.4$
- **B.** $t = -7.4$
- **C.** $t = -14.8$
- **D.** $t = 14.8$

6.NS.5

5. What is the least common multiple of 4 and 8?

- **A.** 1
- **B.** 2
- **C.** 4
- **D.** 8

6.NS.4

6. Bonita had a balance of $104.35 in her bank account at the beginning of the day. By the end of the day her balance was zero. Which statement does NOT explain what could have happened?

- **A.** Bonita withdrew $104.35.
- **B.** Bonita spent $104.35.
- **C.** Bonita deposited $104.35.
- **D.** Bonita borrowed $104.35.

6.NS.5

Five and – 5 are opposites so when they are added together, they have a sum of zero. 5 + (– 5) = 0

1. What is the value of *m* in the equation below?

$m + 3.91 = 0$

- **A.** $m = -3.91$
- **B.** $m = 3.91$
- **C.** $m = 1.96$
- **D.** $m = -1.96$

6.NS.5

2. The Stauffers take a trip from Seattle to San Francisco and back. Their trip takes 8 days. The Arnolds leave at the same time to make the same trip but it takes them 10 days. If the Stauffers and the Arnolds continue to make the trips, how many days will it be before they are both leaving Seattle at the same time?

- **A.** 10 days
- **B.** 20 days
- **C.** 40 days
- **D.** 80 days

6.NS.4

3. Bella was at 645 meters below sea level then she traveled – 811 meters. How many meters should she travel to reach sea level?

- **A.** – 1456 meters
- **B.** 1456 meters
- **C.** – 166 meters
- **D.** 166 meters

6.NS.5

4. What is the GCF of 15, 18 and 33?

- **A.** 1
- **B.** 3
- **C.** 5
- **D.** 6

6.NS.4

5. Bart charged $140 on a credit card. He then charged $53 for dinner. Which action would allow Bart to have zero debt?

- **A.** Bart sent $140 to the credit card company.
- **B.** Bart made a payment of $87.
- **C.** Bart sent $53 to the credit card company.
- **D.** Bart made a payment of $193.

6.NS.5

6. Which expression is modeled by the diagram below?

- **A.** $2\frac{1}{8} \div \frac{1}{4}$
- **B.** $2\frac{1}{8} \div \frac{1}{8}$
- **C.** $\frac{1}{4} \div 2\frac{1}{8}$
- **D.** $\frac{1}{8} \div 2\frac{1}{8}$

6.NS.1

DAY 6
CHALLENGE QUESTION

Chester started tracking a deer at 1,215 yards above sea level. Chester followed the deer down 1,936 yards in altitude then up 60 yards. What altitude will Chester have to travel to get back to sea level?

6.NS.5

24

WEEK 4

ARGOPREP.COM

VIDEO EXPLANATIONS

This week we will look at numbers and see where they lie on a number line. You will also get practice using TWO number lines at the same time. These 2 axes form the rectangular coordinate system.

You can find detailed video explanations to each problem in the book by visiting:
ArgoPrep.com

Use the coordinate system below to answer questions 1 – 5.

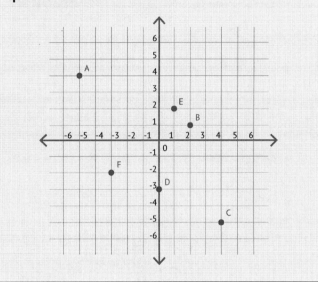

1. What is the y-coordinate of Point E?

   A. 0
   B. 1
   C. 2
   D. 3

6.NS.6

2. What point is located at (4, −5)?

   A. A
   B. C
   C. E
   D. F

6.NS.6

3. Which statement correctly describes the relationship between the origin and Point D?

   A. They are 3 units apart.
   B. It is a reflection across the x-axis.
   C. It is a reflection across the y-axis.
   D. They are 2 units apart.

6.NS.6

4. What are the coordinates for Point D?

   A. (3, 0)   **C.** (−3, 0)
   B. (0, 3)   **D.** (0, −3)

6.NS.6

5. What quadrant would the point with the coordinates (−2, 7) be in?

   A. Quadrant I
   B. Quadrant II
   C. Quadrant III
   D. Quadrant IV

6.NS.6

6. Carmen has 4,596 marbles and she wants to make bags that each contain 24 marbles. How many full bags will she have?

   A. 189   **C.** 191
   B. 190   **D.** 192

6.NS.2

The origin has coordinates (0, 0) and is located where the x and y axes intersect.

26

WEEK 4 · DAY 2

Use the coordinate system below to answer questions 1 – 5.

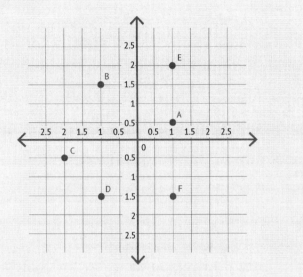

1. Which statement correctly describes the relationship between Point B and Point D?

  A. They are 6 units apart.
  B. It is a reflection across the x-axis.
  C. It is a reflection across the y-axis.
  D. They are 1.5 units apart.   6.NS.6

2. Which point is a reflection of Point F across the y-axis?

  A. A   **C.** D
  B. B   **D.** E   6.NS.6

3. What is the x-coordinate for Point A?

  A. 0.5
  B. 1.0
  C. 1.5
  D. 2.0   6.NS.6

4. What are the coordinates for Point E?

  A. (1, 2)
  B. (2, 1)
  C. (2, 4)
  D. (4, 2)   6.NS.6

5. What quadrant would the point with the coordinates (-0.5, -1.7) be in?

  A. Quadrant I
  B. Quadrant II
  C. Quadrant III
  D. Quadrant IV   6.NS.6

6. Point X is located at (-4, 5). Point Y is a reflection of Point X, reflected across the y-axis. What are the coordinates of Point Y?

  A. (4, -5)
  B. (-4, -5)
  C. (-4, 5)
  D. (4, 5)   6.NS.6

When looking at information on a rectangular coordinate system, be sure to understand the labels for units and the axes.

Cana recorded 5 days of temperatures and her records are shown below. **Use this information to answer questions 1 – 4.**

Day	Temperature (°F)
Monday	– 2 degrees
Tuesday	12 degrees
Wednesday	– 5 degrees
Thursday	14 degrees
Friday	7 degree

1. Cana wants to plot the temperatures on a number line. Which day will be the furthest to the left on the number line?

   A. Monday
   B. Tuesday
   C. Wednesday
   D. Thursday

   6.NS.7

2. Which day had the highest temperature?

   A. Monday
   B. Tuesday
   C. Wednesday
   D. Thursday

   6.NS.7

3. Which day has the largest absolute value?

   A. Monday   C. Wednesday
   B. Tuesday   D. Thursday

   6.NS.7

4. If Cana wanted to only plot the temperatures for Tuesday and Friday, which statement is true?

   A. Cana should plot Tuesday to the left of Friday because 12 < 7.
   B. Cana should plot Tuesday to the left of Friday because 12 > 7.
   C. Cana should plot Friday to the left of Tuesday because 12 < 7.
   D. Cana should plot Friday to the left of Tuesday because 12 > 7.

   6.NS.7

5. The length of Brandon's truck bed is 8 3/4 feet. If the area of the bed is 54 1/4 square feet, what is the width of the truck bed?

   A. $5\frac{7}{8}$ feet   C. $6\frac{3}{4}$ feet

   B. $6\frac{1}{5}$ feet   D. $7\frac{1}{2}$ feet

   6.NS.1

Absolute value is a distance and is always positive. The absolute value of a number is the number's distance from zero.

1. Which of the following statements is TRUE?

    A. $|-12| < -8$
    B. $|-17| > 17$
    C. $|-2| < |1|$
    D. $|-3| > 2$

6.NS.7

Use the following set of numbers to answer questions 2 – 4.

$|-\frac{2}{3}|, -7, |-8|, |1|, 0.5$

---

2. Which number lies furthest to the left on the number line?

    A. $|-\frac{2}{3}|$

    B. -7

    C. $|-8|$

    D. 0.5

6.NS.7

---

3. Which number has the largest value?

    A. $|-\frac{2}{3}|$ **C.** $|-8|$

    B. -7 **D.** 0.5

6.NS.7

---

4. Which number's opposite is positive?

    A. $|-\frac{2}{3}|$ **C.** $|-8|$

    B. -7 **D.** $|1|$

6.NS.7

---

5. There were 3 water bottles. The first bottle was 12.3 inches tall. The second bottle is 8.3 inches shorter than the first one. The third water bottle was 2.5 times as tall as the second bottle. How tall was the third bottle?

    A. 6.5 inches
    B. 10.0 inches
    C. 20.8 inches
    D. 51.5 inches

6.NS.3

---

6. What is $9,519 \div 19$?

    A. 51   **C.** 501
    B. 490   **D.** 511

6.NS.2

The opposite of a number has the same magnitude but a different sign.

Use the rectangular coordinate system below to answer questions 1 – 3.

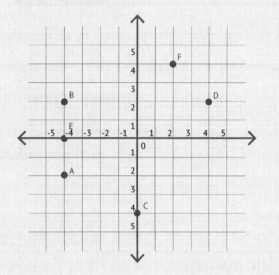

1. Which point has the coordinates (-4,0)?

    A. Point A   **C.** Point D

    B. Point C   **D.** Point E   6.NS.6

2. What are the coordinates of Point B?

    A. (-4, 2)   **C.** (4, 2)

    B. (2, -4)   **D.** (2, 4)   6.NS.6

3. Which point is a reflection of Point A across the x-axis?

    A. Point B   **C.** Point E

    B. Point D   **D.** Point F   6.NS.6

4. Which of the following statements is TRUE?

    A. $12 < -|11|$ **C.** $6 > |-10|$

    B. $|-7| = 7$ **D.** $|5| = -5$ 6.NS.7

Use the following set of numbers to answer questions 5 – 6.

$A = |-3.4|$

$B = 2.8$

$C = |-\frac{1}{2}|$

$D = -5$

$E = |1.4|$

5. Which letter shows a value that is the opposite of − 0.5?

    A. A   **C.** C

    B. B   **D.** E   6.NS.7

6. If the letters above were placed on a number line based on their values, which order below shows how the letters would be arranged from left to right on the number line?

    A. DACEB   **C.** DCEBA

    B. DECAB   **D.** EDCBA   6.NS.7

DAY 6
CHALLENGE QUESTION

Point M is located at (3 - 1). Point N is a reflection of Point M, reflected across the x-axis. What quadrant is Point N in?

   6.NS.6

WEEK 5

VIDEO EXPLANATIONS

ARGOPREP.COM

This week you will get to graph points that represent real numbers in real situations. You will also be able to name the ordered pair that shows the location of a point. Have you ever wondered what an exponent is? Week 5 you will also learn how to write and evaluate numbers that involve exponents.

You can find detailed video explanations to each problem in the book by visiting:
ArgoPrep.com

1. The coordinates of the vertices of a rectangle are A (-2,-3), B (-2, 1), C (2, 1) and D (2,-3). What are the dimensions of the rectangle?

  A. 4 units by 4 units
  B. 2 units by 4 units
  C. 3 units by 2 units
  D. 1 unit by 3 units

6.NS.8

Use the rectangular coordinate system and the parallelogram shown below to answer questions 3 – 4.

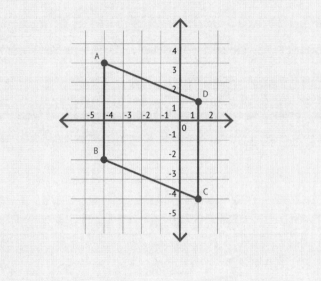

2. A line segment is shown below. What are the endpoints' coordinates?

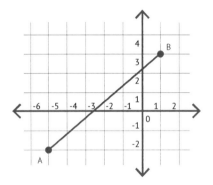

  A. A (-2,-5), B (3, 1)
  B. A (3, 1), B (-2,-5)
  C. A (-5,-2), B (1, 3)
  D. A (1, 3), B (-5,-2)

6.NS.8

3. What is the distance of Line Segment CD?

  A. 4 units   **C.** 6 units
  B. 5 units   **D.** 7 units

6.NS.8

4. What is the distance of Line Segment AB?

  A. 4 units   **C.** 6 units
  B. 5 units   **D.** 7 units

6.NS.8

TIP of the DAY

The distance of anything is always a positive number. Even though a car may travel in reverse, the distance traveled is still positive.

1. The coordinates of the vertices of a rectangle are A (5, 2), B (5, -3), C (-2, 2) and D (-2, -3). What are the dimensions of the rectangle?

- **A.** 3 units by 4 units
- **B.** 4 units by 5 units
- **C.** 5 units by 5 units
- **D.** 7 units by 5 units

6.NS.8

2. What is the greatest common factor of 48 and 76?

- **A.** 2
- **B.** 3
- **C.** 4
- **D.** 12

6.NS.4

3. A line segment is shown below. What are the coordinates of the endpoints?

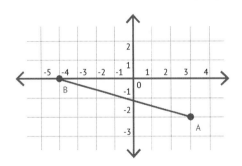

- **A.** A (-2, 3), B (0, -4)
- **B.** A (3, -2), B (-4, 0)
- **C.** A (-4, 0), B (3, -2)
- **D.** A (0, -4), B -2, 3)

6.NS.8

The coordinates of the vertices of a rectangle are A (-1, -3), B (-1, -7), C (4, -7) and D (4, -3). **These coordinates represent a square of material. Use this information to answer questions 4 – 5.**

4. What are the dimensions of the rectangle?

- **A.** 2 units by 3 units
- **B.** 2 units by 10 units
- **C.** 3 units by 10 units
- **D.** 4 units by 5 units

6.NS.8

5. What is the area of the material?

- **A.** 6 units²
- **B.** 10 units²
- **C.** 20 units²
- **D.** 30 units²

6.NS.8

6. What is the least common multiple of 9 and 4?

- **A.** 1
- **B.** 4
- **C.** 18
- **D.** 36

6.NS.4

If a line segment has x-coordinates that are the same, you can determine the length of the segment by finding the absolute value of the difference between the y-coordinates.

1. What is the value of the expression below?

$5^3 - 10$

A. -125
B. 5
C. 115
D. 635

6.EE.1

2. What is the value of the expression below?

$12 + 3^4$

A. 24
B. 93
C. 3,375
D. 50,625

6.EE.1

3. What is the value of the expression below?

$7^2 + \frac{1}{3}(9^2 - 3^2)$

A. 26
B. 53
C. 61
D. 73

6.EE.1

4. What is the value of the expression below?

$50 + 13^2 \times 2$

A. 102
B. 152
C. 388
D. 7,938

6.EE.1

5. What is the value of the expression below?

$18\frac{1}{2} - 2^3 \times \left(4\frac{1}{3} + 6\frac{4}{6}\right)$

A. $-69\frac{1}{2}$ **C.** $-41\frac{1}{2}$

B. $-61\frac{4}{5}$ **D.** $115\frac{1}{2}$

6.EE.1

6. Beatrice and Bertha are walking at the mall. It takes Beatrice 22 minutes to complete a mall loop and it takes Bertha 11 minutes to make a loop. If they start at the same spot and continue walking at a consistent speed, how many minutes will it be until Beatrice and Bertha are both back at their starting point?

A. 2 minutes   **C.** 22 minutes
B. 11 minutes   **D.** 33 minutes

6.NS.4

When finding the value of expressions, be sure to find the value of the exponential numbers before adding or subtracting.

1. What is the value of the expression below?

$6^4 + 107$

- **A.** 131
- **B.** 323
- **C.** 363
- **D.** 1,403

6.EE.1

2. What is the value of the expression below?

$11 - 2^5$

- **A.** – 21
- **B.** – 5
- **C.** 1
- **D.** 59,049

6.EE.1

3. What is the value of the expression below?

$6^3 - \frac{3}{4}(16 - 2^3)$

- **A.** $208\frac{1}{2}$
- **C.** 1,722
- **B.** 210
- **D.** $2,152\frac{1}{2}$

6.EE.1

4. What is the value of the expression below?

$310 - 4^3 \times 3$

- **A.** 118
- **B.** 274
- **C.** 738
- **D.** 894

6.EE.1

5. What is the value of -3^4?

- **A.** – 12
- **B.** 12
- **C.** – 81
- **D.** 81

6.EE.1

6. What is the value of the expression below?

$209\frac{3}{4} - 4^2\left(5^3 - 59\frac{1}{2}\right)$

- **A.** $1,257\frac{3}{4}$
- **C.** $-502\frac{1}{4}$
- **B.** $921\frac{3}{4}$
- **D.** $-838\frac{1}{4}$

6.EE.1

An exponent only applies to what is immediately in front of it.
$(-3)^2 = (-3)(-3) = +9$ but $-3^2 = -(3)(3) = -9$.

35

There is a quadrilateral with the following vertices: A (-2, 0), B (6, 0), C (6, -6) and D (-2, -6). **Use this information to answer questions 1 – 3.**

1. What is the length of Line Segment CD?

A. 2 units
B. 4 units
C. 6 units
D. 8 units

6.NS.8

2. What is the length of Line Segment AD?

A. 2 units
B. 4 units
C. 6 units
D. 8 units

6.NS.8

3. What is the area of the quadrilateral?

A. 16 units²
B. 24 units²
C. 48 units²
D. 64 units²

6.NS.8

4. What is the value of -2^7?

A. -14
B. 14
C. -128
D. 128

6.EE.1

5. What is the value of the expression below?

$$625\tfrac{2}{5} - 3^2 \times \left(3\tfrac{1}{2} + 6^2\right)$$

A. $-186\tfrac{17}{20}$ C. $980\tfrac{9}{10}$

B. $269\tfrac{9}{10}$ D. $1{,}437\tfrac{13}{20}$

6.EE.1

6. What is the value of g in the equation below?

$$45.7 + g = 0$$

A. $g = -47.5$
B. $g = -(-45.7)$
C. $g = 45.7$
D. $g = -45.7$

6.NS.5

DAY 6
CHALLENGE QUESTION

What is the value of the expression below?
$(-1)^2 - 4^2$

6.EE.1

Week 6 you can practice finding if numbers are solutions to equations. Simply substitute in the number, do the operations and if it matches, you have a solution!

You can find detailed video explanations to each problem in the book by visiting:
ArgoPrep.com

1. What is the value of the expression below if $z = 5$?

$z^3 - z$

A. 10
B. 25
C. 70
D. 120

6.EE.2

2. What is the value of the expression below when $a = 2$ and $b = -3$?

$5a - 3b$

A. 1
B. 4
C. 19
D. 43

6.EE.2

3. What is the value of the expression below when $m = 7$ and $n = -11$?

$-8m - n$

A. -45
B. -52
C. -67
D. -74

6.EE.2

4. What is the value of the expression below when $r = \frac{2}{3}$ and $s = -2$?

$-9r - 4s + 3$

A. 1   **C.** -1
B. 5   **D.** -11

6.EE.2

Use the coordinate system below to answer questions 5 – 6.

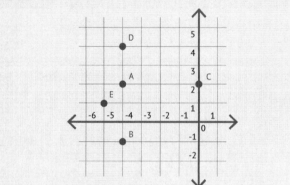

5. What the coordinates for Point B?

A. (-1,-4)   **C.** (1,-4)
B. (-4,-1)   **D.** (-4, 1)

6.NS.6

6. What point is located 3 units from Point A?

A. B   **C.** D
B. C   **D.** E

6.NS.6

To find the value of an equation that has a variable, replace the variable with its value and simplify the equation.

1. What is the value of the expression below if $a = -12$?

$-2a + 14$

A. -10
B. 0
C. 28
D. 38

6.EE.2

4. What is the value of the expression below when $c = -10$ and $d = -8$?

$-5c + d$

A. 58
B. 42
C. -42
D. -58

6.EE.2

2. What is the value of the expression below when $f = -1$ and $g = 6$?

$4f + 3g - 13$

A. 1
B. 17
C. -8
D. -27

6.EE.2

5. Which of the following statements is true?

A. $149.8 + 36 < |149.8 + 36|$

B. $|12 - 21| > |-11|$

C. $0.6 < \frac{2}{3}$

D. $|75| = -|75|$

6.NS.7

3. What is the value of the expression below when $x = 2$ and $y = -1$?

$7x - y^5 + 8$

A. 17
B. 19
C. 21
D. 23

6.EE.2

6. In which quadrant would (5, -2.3) be located?

A. Quadrant I
B. Quadrant II
C. Quadrant III
D. Quadrant IV

6.NS.6

Some students are afraid of variables. Variables are just holding a place in an equation until we can find the missing number.

1. What is the value of the expression below if $k = -2$?

$$-k^3 + k - 6$$

A. -16
B. 0
C. 4
D. 12

6.EE.2

2. What is the value of the expression below when $h = 8.2$ and $j = -3.5$?

$$3h - 5.1j$$

A. -6.65
B. 6.75
C. 29.05
D. 42.45

6.EE.2

3. What is the value of the expression below when $p = -3$ and $q = 6$?

$$12p - q^2 - 7$$

A. -79
B. -65
C. -10
D. -7

6.EE.2v

Davey took 5 tests and he earned an 82 on the first test. The next 4 test scores are shown below in relation to his first test score. **Use this information to answer questions 4 – 5.**

Test	Score (points)
#2	+12
#3	– 8
#4	– 5
#5	+4

4. If Davey's scores were plotted on a number line, which test would be the furthest to the left on that number line?

A. Test #2
B. Test #3
C. Test #4
D. Test #5

6.NS.7

5. Which statement below is NOT true?

A. Test 2 < Test 5
B. Test 3 < Test 1
C. Test 4 > Test 3
D. Test 5 > Test 1

6.NS.7

When a variable has an exponent, only the value of the variable is being squared, cubed, etc. For example, $-k^2$; $k = 3$ means $-k^2 = -(3)(3) = -9$ NOT $(-3)(-3)$.

1. Which of the following expressions is NOT the same as $3(x + 2)$?

A. $2x + 5 + x + 1$
B. $x + x + x + 2 + 4$
C. $3x + 2$
D. $3x + 6$

6.EE.3

4. What is another way to write

$6c + d + 5 - d + 3$?

A. $2(3c - 4)$
B. $6c + 8 - d$
C. $2(3c + 4) - d$
D. $2(3c + 4)$

6.EE.3

2. Which of the following expressions is the same as $r + r + r + r + r$?

A. $r + 5$
B. $5r$
C. $4r$
D. $r + 4$

6.EE.3

5. Point A is located at $(3, -4)$. Point B is a reflection of Point A, reflected across the x-axis. What are the coordinates of Point B?

A. $(3, 4)$
B. $(-3, 4)$
C. $(-4, 3)$
D. $(4, -3)$

6.NS.6

3. Which expression can also be written as $12(3d - 2e)$?

A. $36d - 24e$
B. $36d - 2e$
C. $15d - 122e$
D. $24d - 2e$

6.EE.3

6. The coordinates of the vertices of a rectangle are A $(-5, -1)$, B $(-5, 8)$, C $(1, 8)$ and D $(1, -1)$. What are the dimensions of the rectangle?

A. 6 units by 9 units
B. 8 units by 6 units
C. 13 units by 2 units
D. 16 units by 5 units

6.NS.8

Another way to write $m + m + m + m$ is $4m$.

1. What is the value of the expression below when $m = -4$ and $n = 2.2$?

$6.5n - m$

A. -28.2
B. 10.3
C. 18.3
D. 23.8

6.EE.2

4. Which of the following expressions is the same as $24a + 28b$?

A. $4(6a + 7b)$
B. $3(8a + 9b)$
C. $6(3a + 4b)$
D. $12(2a + 3b)$

6.EE.3

2. What is the value of the expression below when $u = 5.5$ and $v = -2$?

$10u - v^4 + 16$

A. 39
B. 55
C. 71
D. 87

6.EE.2

5. Which of the following expressions is NOT equivalent to the other three?

A. $33a - 12b + 21$
B. $-3(11a - 4b + 7)$
C. $b + 5 - 9a - 24a - 26 + 11b$
D. $-33a + 12d - 21$

6.EE.3

3. Which expression can also be written as $8x(9y - z)$?

A. $72xy - z$
B. $17xy - 8xz$
C. $72xy - 8xz$
D. $17y - 8z$

6.EE.3

6. Which of the following expressions is equivalent to $7c + 5(d - 4) - c$?

A. $5d - 20 - 6c$
B. $5d - 4 - 6c$
C. $6c + 5d - 4$
D. $6c + 5d - 20$

6.EE.3

DAY 6
CHALLENGE
QUESTION

What expression is three times $6x - 9.5y + 4$?   6.EE.3

WEEK 7

VIDEO EXPLANATIONS

ARGOPREP.COM

Sometimes you need to say something a little differently, the same is true for math! Week 7 gives you practice rewriting numbers and algebraic expressions in different ways so they can be useful for different situations.

You can find detailed video explanations to each problem in the book by visiting:
ArgoPrep.com

1. Which of the following expressions is the same as $x + x + x + x - x$?

A. $3x$
B. $4x$
C. $5x$
D. $x + 4$

6.EE.3

2. If a cube has side lengths of $\frac{3}{4}$ - cm, what is the volume of the cube?

A. $\frac{6}{8}$ cm³
C. $\frac{27}{64}$ cm³

B. $\frac{9}{12}$ cm³
D. $\frac{9}{4}$ cm³

6.EE.2

3. What is the surface area of a cube that has side lengths of 4 yards?

A. 48 yds²
B. 48 yds³
C. 96 yds²
D. 96 yds³

6.EE.2

4. If a cube has side lengths of $\frac{1}{3}$ - foot, what is the volume of the cube?

A. $\frac{1}{9}$ ft³
D. $\frac{3}{27}$ ft³

B. $\frac{1}{27}$ ft³

C. $\frac{3}{9}$ ft³

6.EE.2

5. What is the surface area of a cube that has side lengths of 10 cm?

A. 60 cm²
B. 120 cm²
C. 300 cm²
D. 600 cm²

6.EE.2

6. What is the least common multiple of 10 and 12?

A. 2
B. 22
C. 60
D. 120

6.NS.4

To find the surface area of a cube, use the formula $A = 6s^2$.

1. If a cube has side lengths of $3d$ units, what is the volume of the cube?

   A. $9d^2$ units^3
   B. $9d^3$ units^3
   C. $18d^2$ units^3
   D. $27d^3$ units^3

6.EE.2

2. Which of the following expressions is the same as s + s + t + t + s?

   A. st
   B. $5st$
   C. $3s + 2t$
   D. $2t + 15$

6.EE.3

3. Which two expressions are equivalent for any value of a?

   A. $8(a + 2)$ and $8a + 2$
   B. $8(a - 2)$ and $8a - 2$
   C. $8(a + 2)$ and $8a + 16$
   D. $8a - 2$ and $2(4a - 2)$

6.EE.4

The coordinates of the vertices of a rectangle are A (1, -3), B (5, -3), C (5, 1) and D (1, 1). **Use this information to answer questions 4 – 5.**

4. What are the dimensions of the rectangle?

   A. 5 units by 2 units
   B. 4 units by 4 units
   C. 3 units by 5 units
   D. 2 units by 4 units

6.NS.8

5. What is the length of Line Segment BC?

   A. 1 unit
   B. 3 units
   C. 4 units
   D. 5 units

6.NS.8

6. What is the value of the expression below?

$$4 + 8^2 \times 2$$

   A. 132
   B. 136
   C. 288
   D. 512

6.EE.1

The volume of a cube can be found by using the formula V = s^3.

TIP of the DAY

1. What is the surface area of a cube that has side lengths of 3.5 cm?

A. 42 cm²
B. 73.5 cm²
C. 147 cm²
D. 441 cm²

6.EE.2

4. Which of the following expressions is the same as $7u \times 7u \times 7u \times 7u \times 7u$?

A. $5 \times 7u$
B. $(7u)^5$
C. $7u \times 5$
D. $7u^5$

6.EE.3

2. Which two expressions are equivalent for any value of x?

A. $5x + 25$ and $5(x + 20)$
B. $5(x - 1)$ and $5x - 1$
C. $(x + 5)$ and $x - 5$
D. $10 - 5x$ and $5(2 - x)$

6.EE.4

5. Which two expressions are equivalent for any value of a and b?

A. $14ab + 24a$ and $2a(7b + 12)$
B. $9ab + 14a$ and $2a(7b + 12)$
C. $24a + 14b$ and $2a(7b + 12)$
D. $9ab + 24a$ and $2a(7b + 12)$

6.EE.4

3. If a cube has side lengths of $\frac{2}{5}$ yard, what is the volume of the cube?

A. $\frac{6}{15}$ yd³   **D.** $\frac{8}{125}$ yd³

B. $\frac{8}{75}$ yd³

C. $\frac{6}{125}$ yd³

6.EE.2

6. What is the greatest common factor of 49 and 98?

A. 7
B. 14
C. 21
D. 49

6.NS.4

Two expressions are equivalent if when a number is substituted in for a variable, the two expressions have the same result.

1. If a cube has side lengths of $\frac{1}{2}$ - inch, what is the volume of the cube?

   A. $\frac{1}{8}$ in³   **D.** $\frac{3}{6}$ in³

   B. $\frac{1}{6}$ in³

   C. $\frac{3}{8}$ in³

6.EE.2

4. Which two expressions are equivalent for any value of c?

   A. $c^3 + c$ and $c\,(c^2 + 1)$
   B. $c + c + c$ and c^3
   C. $c \times c \times c$ and $3c$
   D. $c\,(c + 1)$ and $c + c$

6.EE.4

2. Which two expressions are equivalent for any value of w?

   A. $w + w + w + w$ and $w + 4$
   B. $w + w + w + w$ and $4w$
   C. $w + w + w + w$ and w^4
   D. $w \times w \times w \times w$ and $4w$

6.EE.4

5. If a cube has side lengths of $2t$ units, what is the volume of the cube?

   A. $2t^3$ units³
   B. $6t^3$ units³
   C. $8t$ units³
   D. $8t^3$ units³

6.EE.2

3. What is the surface area of a cube that has side lengths of $6y$ cm?

   A. $18y^3$ cm²
   B. $36y^2$ cm²
   C. $216y^2$ cm²
   D. $216y^3$ cm²

6.EE.2

6. What is the value of the expression below when $a = 4.5$ and $b = -2$?

$7a - 6b + 2$

   A. 1.5
   B. 21.5
   C. 35.5
   D. 45.5

6.EE.2

To determine if 2 expressions are equivalent you can use the Associative, Commutative and/or Distributive Properties.

1. What is the surface area of a cube that has side lengths of 2.1 inches?

   A. 26.46 in²
   B. 37.8 in²
   C. 132.3 in²
   D. 158.76 in²

6.EE.2

2. Which two expressions are equivalent for any value of z?

   A. $18z - 2$ and $6(3z - 2)$
   B. $3(2z - 4)$ and $6(z - 2)$
   C. $3z(2z - 4)$ and $6z - 12z$
   D. $6z - 2$ and $6(z - 2)$

6.EE.4

3. If a cube has side lengths of $7a$ units, what is the volume of the cube?

   A. $49a^3$ units³
   B. $21a^3$ units³
   C. $343a^3$ units³
   D. $147a^3$ units³

6.EE.2

4. What is another way to write *"six less than m"*?

   A. $m - 6$
   B. $6 - m$
   C. $m \div 6$
   D. $6 + m$

6.EE.2

5. What is the value of f in the equation below?

$0 = -31.8 + f$

   A. $f = 31.8$
   B. $f = -31.8$
   C. $f = 31.8f$
   D. $f = -31.8f$

6.NS.5

6. In which quadrant would (-8, -1) be located?

   A. Quadrant I
   B. Quadrant II
   C. Quadrant III
   D. Quadrant IV

6.NS.6

DAY 6
CHALLENGE QUESTION

Use the Distributive Property to find an expression that is equivalent to $5(a - 4) - 2(7 - b)$

6.EE.3

For Week 8 you are given some numbers and you will have a chance to find out which ones are solutions, to make an equation (or inequality) true.

You can find detailed video explanations to each problem in the book by visiting: ArgoPrep.com

1. The set of numbers 2, 5, 8 and 18 contains values for x. What value of x makes the equation below true?

$3x + 12 = 18$

A. 2
B. 5
C. 8
D. 18

6.EE.5

2. Which equation is true when $y = 7$?

A. $\frac{y}{14} = 2$

B. $13 - 2y = -1$

C. $y + 3 = 11$

D. $-5y = -28$

6.EE.5

3. Which equation has the solution:

$a = -12$?

A. $4a + 3 = -45$
B. $a + 4 = 8$
C. $5a = -62$
D. $10a - 9 = -132$

6.EE.5

4. What is the smallest integer value for n that would make $n + 8 > 15$ true?

A. 6
B. 7
C. 8
D. 9

6.EE.5

5. Which two expressions are equivalent for any value of x?

A. $3(x + 1)$ and $3x + 1$
B. $x + x + x$ and x^3
C. $3(x - 1)$ and $3x - 3$
D. $(x)(x)(x)$ and $3x$

6.EE.4

6. Using the formula $F = 1.8C + 32$, what is the temperature in degrees Fahrenheit when it is 18°C?

A. 22.4°F
B. 42.0°F
C. 51.8°F
D. 64.4°F

6.EE.2

A number is a solution to an equation if it makes the equation true.

1. Which equation has the solution:

$b = -1$?

A. $2b + 5 = -3$ **D.** $6b - 2 = -8$

B. $\frac{-11}{b} = -11$

C. $8 - b = 7$

6.EE.5

4. Which equation is true when $r = 5$?

A. $r + 2 = 10$
B. $-4r = 20$
C. $-8 - r = -13$
D. $2r - 3 = 4$

6.EE.5

2. What is the largest integer value for x that would make $x + 11 < -3$ true?

A. -16
B. -15
C. -14
D. -13

6.EE.5

5. Which two expressions are equivalent for any value of z?

A. $4z - 8$ and $2(2z - 4)$
B. $z + z + z + z$ and z^4
C. $4(z + 4)$ and $4z + 4$
D. $3z^3$ and $3z + 3z + 3z$

6.EE.4

3. The set of numbers -4, 2, 8 and 16 contains values for v. What value of v makes the equation below true?

$\frac{v}{4} - 2 = 0$

A. -4
B. 2
C. 8
D. 16

6.EE.5

6. What is the value of the expression below if $b = -11$?

$25 - b$

A. 14
B. 26
C. 34
D. 36

6.EE.2

To determine if a value is a solution to an equation, substitute in the value and see if the number makes the equation true.

The set of h is shown below. **Use its elements to find the solutions for the equations in questions 1 – 3.**

$h = \{-5, 4, 5, 20\}$

The set of m is shown below. **Use its elements to find the solutions for the equations in questions 4, 5.**

$m = \{-1, 3, 5, -2, 0\}$

1. Which element of h is the solution to: $4h = -20$?

A. -5
B. 4
C. 5
D. 20

6.EE.5

4. Which element/s of m is/are the solution/s to: $7m - 2 < -2$?

A. $-1, -2$
B. $0, -1, -2$
C. $5, -1, 3$
D. $3, 0, -2$

6.EE.5

2. Which element of h is the solution to: $12 - h = -8$?

A. -5
B. 4
C. 5
D. 20

6.EE.5

5. Which element/s of m is/are the solution/s to: $4m > -8$?

A. $-1, 0, 3$
B. $0, -1, 3, 5$
C. $5, -1, -2, 3,$
D. $3, 0, -2, 5, -1$

6.EE.5

3. Which element of h is the solution to: $7h + 3 = 38$?

A. -5 **D.** 20
B. 4
C. 5

6.EE.5

6. What is $4,706 \div 26$?

A. 171
B. 181
C. 191
D. 201

6.NS.2

When looking for solutions to inequalities, often the inequality has more than 1 possible answer that makes the inequality true.

1. The set of numbers 9, 10, 15 and 18 contains values for q. What value of q makes the equation below true?

$\frac{q}{3} - 8 = -2$

A. 9
B. 10
C. 15
D. 18

6.EE.5

2. Which equation is true when $d = -3$?

A. $-6d = -18$
B. $d^2 - 8 = 1$
C. $d + 7 = -4$
D. $4 - d = 1$

6.EE.5

3. Which equation has the solution $j = -1$

A. $4j - 2 = -6$
B. $3j = 3$
C. $5 - j = 4$
D. $8 - j^2 = 9$

6.EE.5

4. What is the largest integer value for z that would make $3z + 1 < -8$ true?

A. -2
B. -3
C. -4
D. -5

6.EE.5

5. Casey bought 8 peaches. If p represents the cost for 1 peach, which expression shows the cost of 8 peaches?

A. $p + 8$ **C.** $p - 8$

B. $8p$ **D.** $\frac{p}{8}$

6.EE.6

6. Each package of bacon is $4.49. If Chaz bought b packages of bacon, what expression represents the cost of all of the bacon he bought?

A. $b + 4.49$ **C.** $4.49b$

B. $b - 4.49$ **D.** $\frac{b}{4.49}$

6.EE.6

Remember when a negative number is being subtracted, it is the same result as if a positive number were being added. For example, 7 – (–2) = 7 + 2.

1. The set of numbers − 6, 5, 12 and 21 contains values for k. What value of k makes the equation below true?

$$\frac{k}{3} - 6 = -2$$

A. − 6
B. 5
C. 12
D. 21

6.EE.5

4. What is the smallest integer value for n that would make $-8n \leq -24$ true?

A. − 2
B. − 3
C. 3
D. 4

6.EE.5

2. Which equation is NOT true when:

$y = -5$?

A. $10 - y = 15$
B. $y + 5 = 0$
C. $13 - 5y = 38$
D. $-6y = -30$

6.EE.5

5. Which equation has the solution $j = 0$?

A. $4j + 5 = -5$

B. $3j = 3$

C. $3j + 1 = 1$

D. $\frac{j}{3} = 1$

6.EE.5

3. Which two expressions are equivalent for any value of a?

A. $7a - 21$ and $7(a - 3)$
B. $7(a - 3)$ and $7a - 3$
C. $4a^2$ and $(4a)^2$
D. $7(3a)$ and $10a$

6.EE.4

6. Which of the following statements is TRUE?

A. $32.5 < |-30|$
B. $-|-40.8| \geq |-40.8|$
C. $19 - 8 > |-72|$
D. $|12 - 36| > -24$

6.NS.7

DAY 6
CHALLENGE QUESTION

Cassandra is C years old. If her sister is 5 years younger than Cassandra, how old is her sister?

6.EE.6

54

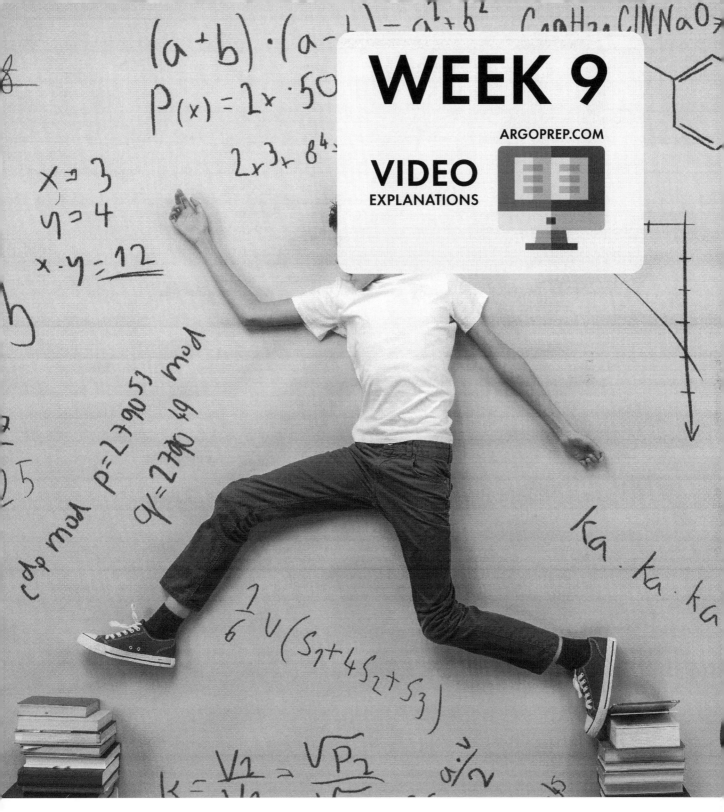

This week you can practice writing your own algebraic expressions by comparing one quantity to another to form a relationship equation.

You can find detailed video explanations to each problem in the book by visiting:
ArgoPrep.com

1. What is the largest integer value for f that would make $11 - f > -2$ true?

   A. 11
   B. 12
   C. 13
   D. 14

6.EE.5

2. Which two expressions are equivalent for any value of g?

   A. $g + g + g$ and g^3
   B. $g(1 - g)$ and $g^2 - g$
   C. $g - g$ and $0g$
   D. $g(g - 1)$ and $2g - g$

6.EE.4

3. Which equation has the solution $s = -\frac{1}{2}$?

   A. $8s = 4$
   B. $5s = -2.5$
   C. $2s - 1 = -1$
   D. $s(4 + 2) = 3$

6.EE.5

Traci is t years old. **Use this information to answer questions 4 – 6.**

4. Scott is 1 year older than Traci. How old is Scott?

   A. $t + 1$
   B. $t - 1$
   C. $1t$
   D. $t \div 1$

6.EE.6

5. Jeanne is three times as old as Traci. How old is Jeanne?

   A. $t + 3$
   B. $t - 3$
   C. $3t$
   D. $t \div 3$

6.EE.6

6. Lee is 5 years younger than Traci. How old is Lee?

   A. $t + 5$
   B. $t - 5$
   C. $5t$
   D. $t \div 5$

6.EE.6

It is important to choose a variable that will have some meaning. For example, if you are trying to find the number of birds, you may wish to choose b to represent that number.

1. Dallas put g gallons of gas in his car. If the car holds 21 gallons to begin, which expression tells how much gas was in the car before Dallas bought gas?

   A. $21 - g$
   B. $g - 21$
   C. $21 + g$
   D. $21 \times g$

6.EE.6

2. The length of the couch is 4 feet longer than the chair, which is c feet long. How long is the couch?

   A. $c + 4$ feet
   B. $c - 4$ feet
   C. $c \times 4$ feet
   D. $c \div 4$ feet

6.EE.6

3. The deck is 1/2 as wide as it is long. If the deck is d meters long, how wide is the deck?

   A. $d + \frac{1}{2}$ **C.** $d - \frac{1}{2}$

   B. $d \div \frac{1}{2}$ **D.** $d \times \frac{1}{2}$

6.EE.6

4. Which two expressions are equivalent for any value of p?

   A. $p - 2 + p$ and $p^2 - 2$
   B. $8p - 3p$ and $5p$
   C. $p \times p \times p$ and $3p$
   D. $5p\,(p + 1)$ and $6p + 5p$

6.EE.4

5. Donald's car is three times as long as his bike. If his bike is b, what is the length of Donald's car?

   A. $b + 3$
   B. $b - 3$
   C. $3b$
   D. $b \div 3$

6.EE.6

6. What is the surface area of a cube that has side lengths of 7 cm?

   A. 252 cm²
   B. 294 cm²
   C. 343 cm²
   D. 2,058 cm²

6.EE.2

When finding more than one number, use the same variable, but in relation to each number.

WEEK 9 · DAY 3

The apples cost *a* dollars. **Use this information to answer questions 1 – 3.**

The coordinates of the vertices of a rectangle are A (-7,-2), B (-1,-2), C (-1,-5) and D (-7,-5). **Use this information to answer questions 4 – 5.**

1. The bananas cost 2 dollars less than the apples. How much did the bananas cost?

   A. $2 - a$ **C.** $\frac{1}{2}a$

   B. $2a$ **D.** $a - 2$

   6.EE.6

4. What are the dimensions of the rectangle?

   A. 2 units by 5 units
   B. 3 units by 6 units
   C. 5 units by 3 units
   D. 7 units by 2 units

   6.NS.8

2. The oranges cost twice as much as the apples. How much did the oranges cost?

   A. $2 - a$ **C.** $\frac{1}{2}a$

   B. $2a$ **D.** $a - 2$

   6.EE.6

5. What is the length of Line Segment BC?

   A. 2 units
   B. 3 units
   C. 5 units
   D. 6 units

   6.NS.8

3. The peaches cost half as much as the apples. How much did the peaches cost?

   A. $2 - a$ **C.** $\frac{1}{2}a$

   B. $2a$ **D.** $a - 2$

   6.EE.6

6. What is the least common multiple of 4 and 6?

   A. 1
   B. 2
   C. 12
   D. 24

   6.NS.4

A variable can have different values but only one value at a time. For example, x = 4 in x + 3 = 7 but x = -2 in 5x = -10.

1. Which equation has the solution $u = -\frac{1}{3}$?

A. $8u = -2\frac{2}{3}$ **D.** $6u = 2$

B. $u + 3 = 3\frac{1}{3}$

C. $7 - u = 6\frac{2}{3}$ 6.EE.5

---

4. Calla baked c cupcakes and Desmond made twice as many cupcakes as Calla. How many cupcakes did Desmond bake?

A. $c + 2$ **C.** $2c$

B. $c - 2$ **D.** $\frac{1}{2}c$

6.EE.6

---

2. The temperature today is t degrees. It is 12 degrees warmer than yesterday. What was yesterday's temperature?

A. $t + 12$
B. $t - 12$
C. $12t$
D. $12 - t$

6.EE.6

Drew is d inches tall. **Use this information to answer questions 5 – 6.**

5. Evelyn is $\frac{1}{2}$ as tall as Drew. How tall is Evelyn?

A. $\frac{1}{2}d$ inches   **C.** $2 + d$ inches

B. $2d$ inches   **D.** $2 - d$ inches

6.EE.6

---

3. Esme ran m miles, which was 4 times as much as Esther ran. How far did Esther run?

A. $m + 4$ miles   **C.** $\frac{1}{4}m$ miles

B. $m - 4$ miles   **D.** $4m$ miles

6.EE.6

---

6. Erik is 2 inches taller than Drew. How tall is Erik?

A. $\frac{1}{2}d$ inches   **C.** $2 + d$ inches

B. $2d$ inches   **D.** $2 - d$ inches

6.EE.6

Remember that when two negative numbers are multiplied or divided, the result is a positive number.

59

1. The Cowboys scored p points, which was 10 less points than the Indians. How many points did the Indians score?

A. $p + 10$
B. $p - 10$
C. $10 - p$
D. $10p$

6.EE.6

4. The length of the wall is w feet, which is 4 times the width. What is the width of the wall?

A. $\frac{1}{4}w$ feet   **D.** $w - 4$ feet

B. $4w$ feet

C. $w + 4$ feet

6.EE.6

2. Chuck ate d donuts yesterday, which was half as much as he ate today. How many donuts did Chuck eat today?

A. $d + 2$ **C.** $\frac{1}{2}d$

B. $d - 2$ **D.** $2d$

6.EE.6

5. What is another way to write *"the quotient of 6 and s"*?

A. $6 + s$ **D.** $\frac{6}{s}$

B. $6 - s$

C. $6s$

6.EE.2

3. Chelsea scored g goals today, which was 3 more goals than they scored last game. How many goals did Chelsea score last game?

A. $g + 3$ **C.** $3g$

B. $g - 3$ **D.** $\frac{1}{3}g$

6.EE.6

6. If a cube has side lengths of $11n$ units, what is the volume of the cube?

A. $11n^3$ units^3
B. $22n^3$ units^3
C. $121n^3$ units^3
D. $1{,}331n^3$ units^3

6.EE.2

DAY 6
CHALLENGE QUESTION

There is a square that has an area that is $144b^2$ square centimeters. What is the length of the square and what is the perimeter of the square?

6.EE.6

In Week 10 you have an opportunity to write your own equations or inequalities to make them fit any situation you are given. Inequalities allow you the chance to have answers that include more than one number.

You can find detailed video explanations to each problem in the book by visiting:
ArgoPrep.com

WEEK 10 · DAY I

ARGOPREP.COM

Evie spent $21 to buy 5 pairs of socks. S represents a pair of socks. **Use this information to answer questions 1 – 2.**

Eduardo purchased 8 packages of candy for $28.72. **Use c to represent a package of candy. Use this information to answer questions 3 – 4.**

1. Which equation could be used to find the cost of 1 pair of socks?

A. $21S = 5$
B. $5S = 21$
C. $S + 5 = 21$
D. $S + 21 = 5$

6.EE.7

2. What was the cost for one pair of socks?

A. $3.90
B. $4.20
C. $4.25
D. $4.45

6.EE.7

3. Which equation could be used to find the cost of a package of candy?

A. $28.72 = 8 + c$ **C.** $28.72 + c = 8$
B. $28.72c = 8$ **D.** $28.72 = 8c$

6.EE.7

4. What was the cost for one package of candy?

A. $3.19   **C.** $3.59
B. $3.39   **D.** $3.79

6.EE.7

5. What is the solution to this equation: $7w = 45.5$?

A. $w = 6.5$ **C.** $w = 7.1$
B. $w = 6.8$ **D.** $w = 7.3$

6.EE.7

6. Express "*h less than 8*" as an algebraic expression.

A. $h - 8$ **C.** $\frac{1}{8} h - 8$

B. $8 - h$ **D.** $8 - \frac{1}{8} h$

6.EE.2

To find a solution to a word problem, sometimes it is important to find the correct equation first.

Elsa walked k kilometers in the park. **Use this information to answer questions 1 – 4.**

1. Fred walked 6 km less than Elsa. How far did Fred walk?

A. $k - 6$ **C.** $\frac{1}{6} k$

B. $6 - k$ **D.** $\frac{k}{6}$

6.EE.6

2. If Elsa walked 15 km, how far did Fred walk?

A. 3 km
B. 6 km
C. 9 km
D. 12 km

6.EE.7

3. Together Frannie and Elsa walked 24 km. How far did Frannie walk?

A. $k - 24$
B. $24 - k$
C. $k + 24$
D. $k + f$

6.EE.6

4. Elsa walked 12 km less than Ernest. How far did Ernest walk?

A. $k + 12$

B. $k - 12$

C. $12 - k$

D. $\frac{1}{12} k$

6.EE.6

5. What is the solution to this equation: $a - 8.5 = 10$?

A. $a = 1.5$
B. $a = 11.5$
C. $a = 18.5$
D. $a = 20$

6.EE.7

6. Greg's heart rate was no more than 71 beats. Which inequality shows how many beats, b, Greg's heart had?

A. $b > 71$
B. $b < 71$
C. $b \geq 71$
D. $b \leq 71$

6.EE.8

When showing an inequality on a number line, if the dot is colored in, then that point is included in the solution.

1. Gayle slept less than 7 hours Tuesday. Which inequality shows how many hours, h, Gayle slept?

A. $h > 7$
B. $h < 7$
C. $h \geq 7$
D. $h \leq 7$

6.EE.8

2. There are 51 students on 3 buses. Which equation could be used to find the number of students, s, on one bus?

A. $s + 3 = 51$
B. $s - 3 = 51$
C. $3s = 51$
D. $3 \div s = 51$

6.EE.7

3. What is the solution to this equation:
$\frac{1}{3} v = 4$?

A. $v = \frac{3}{4}$ **D.** $v = 15$

B. $v = \frac{4}{3}$

C. $v = 12$

6.EE.7

4. The elevator can only hold less than 2500 pounds. There are already people on it that have a combined weight of 1,968 pounds. How much more weight, w, can the elevator manage?

A. $w > 4{,}468$
B. $w < 4{,}468$
C. $w > 532$
D. $w < 532$

6.EE.8

5. To pass the class, Georgia must score at least an 81 on her next test. If her next test is t, which inequality shows the score Georgia will need to pass?

A. $t > 81$
B. $t < 81$
C. $t \geq 81$
D. $t \leq 81$

6.EE.8

6. What inequality is shown on the number line below?

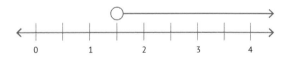

A. $n > 1.5$ **C.** $n \geq 1.5$
B. $n < 1.5$ **D.** $n \leq 1.5$

6.EE.8

If a solution is greater than 4 (> 4), it does NOT include 4 but it is any number larger than 4.

1. There are 68 dogs at the kennel. They are kept in 4 different areas. Which equation could be used to find the number of dogs, d, in one area?

   A. $d = 68 + 4$
   B. $d = 68 - 4$
   C. $d = 68 \times 4$
   D. $d = 68 \div 4$

   6.EE.7

2. To make the team, Heather must run her distance faster than 99 seconds. Which inequality shows the time, t, Heather must run to make the team?

   A. $t < 99$
   B. $t > 99$
   C. $t \leq 99$
   D. $t \geq 99$

   6.EE.8

3. What inequality is shown on the number line below?

   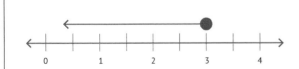

   A. $n > 3$ C. $n \geq 3$
   B. $n < 3$ D. $n \leq 3$

   6.EE.8

4. To pass the class, Glen must get less than 13 wrong on his exam. If his exam is e, which inequality shows the number Glen can get wrong and still pass?

   A. $e > 13$
   B. $e < 13$
   C. $e \geq 13$
   D. $e \leq 13$

   6.EE.8

5. What is the solution to this equation:

   $b + 6 = 13$?

   A. $b = 7$
   B. $b = 11$
   C. $b = 19$
   D. $b = 23$

   6.EE.7

6. Express *"2 less than 3 times x"* as an algebraic expression.

   A. $2 - 3x$
   B. $3x - 2$
   C. $2 - x^3$
   D. $x^3 - 2$

   6.EE.2

When showing an inequality on a number line, if the dot is NOT colored in, or is just a circle, then that point is NOT a part of the solution.

1. Francisco drove at least 16.5 hours yesterday. Which inequality shows how many hours, h, Francisco drove?

   A. $h > 16.5$
   B. $h < 16.5$
   C. $h \geq 16.5$
   D. $h \leq 16.5$

   6.EE.8

2. Gabby used 50 paper towels to clean up the mess. If the roll originally had 250 sheets, how many paper towels are left?

   A. 100
   B. 200
   C. 300
   D. 400

   6.EE.7

3. In order to ride the roller coaster, a person has to be at least 48 inches tall. Which inequality shows how tall, t, a person must be to ride the roller coaster?

   A. $t < 48$
   B. $t > 48$
   C. $t \leq 48$
   D. $t \geq 48$

   6.EE.8

4. What is the largest integer value for n that would make $n - 5 \leq 13$ true?

   A. 8
   B. 11
   C. 18
   D. 23

   6.EE.5

5. What is the solution for $\frac{3}{4} k = 8$?

   A. $k = 6$
   C. $k = 8\frac{3}{4}$
   B. $k = 7\frac{1}{4}$
   D. $k = 10\frac{2}{3}$

   6.EE.7

6. Dylan has 3 times as many pennies as he needs. If he has 111 pennies, which equation could be used to find p, the number of pennies needed?

   A. $3p = 111$
   B. $p \div 3 = 111$
   C. $p = 111 + 3$
   D. $p = 111 - 3$

   6.EE.7

DAY 6
CHALLENGE QUESTION

Write the inequality for x that is shown below.

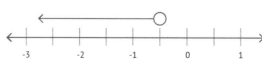

6.EE.8

66

In Week 11 you will practice using 2 variables that change in relation to each other. These are called dependent variables and have a consistent relationship with one another. You will also explore ratios.

You can find detailed video explanations to each problem in the book by visiting:
ArgoPrep.com

1. Which equation is represented in the data from the chart below?

x	y
5	7.5
4	6
2	3

A. $y = 1.5x$
B. $x = 1.5y$
C. $y = 2.5x$
D. $x = 2.5y$

6.EE.9

2. At the thrift shop Hartley bought 5 shirts for $12. Which equation shows the relationship between the number of shirts, s, and C, the total cost for the shirts?

A. $12s = 5C$
B. $2.4s = C$
C. $2.4C = s$
D. $5s = 12C$

6.EE.9

3. Tickets are priced at $65 each. Which equation shows the relationship between C, the cost of the tickets and t, the number of tickets?

A. $t = 65 + C$
B. $C = 65 + t$
C. $t = 65C$
D. $C = 65t$

6.EE.9

The graph below shows the number of hats, h, (horizontal axis) and their cost, C, (on the vertical axis). **Use this information shown below to answer questions 4 – 5.**

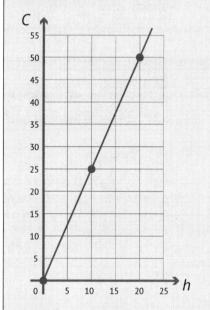

4. Which equation is shown in the above graph?

A. $C = 2.5h$ C. $C = 10h$
B. $2.5C = h$ D. $25C = h$

6.EE.9

5. What is most likely the cost if 12 hats are purchased?

A. $10   C. $30
B. $20   D. $40

6.EE.9

Two quantities that change in relation to each other have a relationship with one another.

1. Grace drove 264 miles, m, on 12 gallons of gas, g. Which equation shows the relationship between the number of miles driven and the gallons of gas?

A. $264m = g$
B. $12g = m$
C. $g = 22m$
D. $m = 22g$

6.EE.9

2. Which equation is represented in the data from the chart below?

x	y
3	1
9	3
12	4

A. $y = x - 2$

B. $x = y - 2$

C. $y = \frac{1}{3}x$

D. $x = \frac{1}{3}y$

6.EE.9

3. The speed limit, s, means that is the maximum speed you can travel without receiving a ticket. If the speed limit is 55 miles per hour (mph), which speed is most likely to keep you from receiving a ticket?

A. $s > 55$ **C.** $s < 55$
B. $s \geq 55$ **D.** $s \leq 55$

6.EE.8

4. Which value(s) of Set P are true for the equation $2P > 7$?

$P = \{-2, -1, 3, 5, 6\}$

A. $-1, 3, 5, 6$
B. $-2, 3, 5$
C. $5, 6$
D. 6

6.EE.5

5. Eugene works 3 hours more than Dudley. If Eugene works h hours, how many hours does Dudley work?

A. $h + 3$
B. $h - 3$
C. $3h$
D. $h \div 3$

6.EE.6

6. Which equation is represented in the data from the chart below?

x	y
2	3
4	5
5	6

A. $y = x + 1$

B. $x = y + 1$

C. $y = \frac{2}{3}x$

D. $x = \frac{2}{3}y$

6.EE.9

If you have an equation, as long as you have one of the numbers, you can substitute it into the equation to find any missing variables.

Below are some people who attended a play. **Use this table below to answer questions 1 – 5.**

Adults (ages 13 – 60 years)	30
Youth (ages 2 – 12 years)	15
Seniors (ages over 60 years)	12
Babies (ages under 2 years)	3

3. What is the ratio of youth to adults?

  A. 1:2
  B. 2:1
  C. 2:5
  D. 5:2

6.RP.1

1. What is the ratio of youth to babies?

  A. 1:3
  B. 1:5
  C. 3:1
  D. 5:1

6.RP.1

4. What is the ratio of seniors to babies?

  A. 1:3
  B. 1:4
  C. 3:1
  D. 4:1

6.RP.1

2. What is the ratio of seniors to adults?

  A. 1:2
  B. 2:1
  C. 2:5
  D. 5:2

6.RP.1

5. What is the ratio of babies to all those who attended the play?

  A. 1:10
  B. 1:20
  C. 10:1
  D. 20:1

6.RP.1

In ratios, the order matters. 12:5 is not the same as 5:12.

Below are the number of times 4 rides at the amusement park were run during the day. **Use this table below to answer questions 1 – 4.**

Tippy Teacups	35
Purple Pony Pirates	27
Fantastic Flyers	50
Tilt-N-Hurl	63

3. What is the ratio of times the Purple Pony Pirates was run compared to the Tilt-N-Hurl?

A. 3:7
B. 5:7
C. 5:9
D. 9:20

6.RP.1

1. What is the ratio of times the Tilt-N-Hurl was run compared to the Tippy Teacups?

A. 5:8
B. 5:9
C. 8:5
D. 9:5

6.RP.1

4. What is the ratio of times the Fantastic Flyers was run compared to the other rides?

A. 1:7
B. 2:5
C. 2:7
D. 5:2

6.RP.1

2. What is the ratio of times the Purple Pony Pirates was run compared to the Tippy Teacups?

A. 2:3
B. 3:4
C. 4:5
D. 27:35

6.RP.1

5. Liza ran $\frac{1}{2}$ as fast as Felicia. If Liza had a speed of L, what was Felicia's speed?

A. $\frac{1}{2}L$ D. $2 - L$

B. $2L$

C. $2 + L$

6.EE.6

Ratios should be reduced so 8:4 would be written as 2:1.

WEEK II · DAY 5
ASSESSMENT

1. There were 9 red shirts for every 6 blue shirts. What is the ratio of blue shirts to red shirts?

A. 1:3
B. 2:3
C. 3:1
D. 3:2

6.RP.1

4. The ratio of oranges to apples is 1:4. If there are 8 apples, how many oranges are there?

A. 2
B. 16
C. 24
D. 32

6.RP.1

2. Which equation is represented in the data from the chart below?

x	y
4	5
2	2.5
6	7.5

A. $y = 1.5x$
B. $y = 1.25x$
C. $y = x + 1$
D. $y = x + 1.5$

6.EE.9

5. Which equation is represented in the data from the chart below?

x	y
0.5	2
2	8
2.5	1

A. $x = 4y$

B. $y = 4x$

C. $y = \frac{1}{4} x$

D. $x = \frac{1}{4} y$

3. Each pint of blueberries is \$3.78. Which equation could be used to find the cost, C, of p pints of blueberries?

A. $p = 3.78C$
B. $p = C + 3.78$
C. $C = p + 3.78$
D. $C = 3.78p$

6.EE.9

6.EE.9

DAY 6
CHALLENGE QUESTION

Using the table from #5, if $x = 3$, what would be the value of y?

6.EE.9

During Week 12, you will further your knowledge of ratios by studying unit rates to solve real-world problems using tables and percents.

You can find detailed video explanations to each problem in the book by visiting:
ArgoPrep.com

WEEK 12 · DAY 1

ARGOPREP.COM

1. If Jerica spent $1,225 on 25 pairs of shoes, what was the cost of 1 pair?

A. $47
B. $49
C. $51
D. $53

6.RP.2

4. A container of oil was $15.79 and it contained 7.5 quarts of oil. How much was 1 quart of oil?

A. $1.99
B. $2.03
C. $2.08
D. $2.11

6.RP.2

2. If 10 loaves of bread require 8 cups of flour, how many cups of flour are in 1 loaf of bread?

A. $\frac{4}{5}$ cups   D. 2 cups

B. $\frac{5}{4}$ cups

C. $\frac{3}{2}$ cups

6.RP.2

5. For 2 hours every day for 3 weeks Harrison swims laps in the pool. If he swims 630 laps in those 3 weeks, how many laps does Harrison swim per hour?

A. 13
B. 14
C. 15
D. 16

6.RP.2

3. A 12 ounce can of soda cost $0.72. What is the unit rate for the soda?

A. $0.60/ounce
B. $0.17/ounce
C. $0.06/ounce
D. $0.05/ounce

6.RP.2

6. Elena is making a batch of soap. It calls for 12 cups of borax and 54 ounces of bar soap. If Elena only had 1 cup of borax, how many ounces of bar soap would she use?

A. 3.5 ounces
B. 4.5 ounces
C. 5.0 ounces
D. 6.5 ounces

6.RP.2

The unit rate is the amount of money (or time or other unit) per ONE thing. Miles per hour is a unit rate because it tells the number of miles a person travels in ONE hour.

1. Heidi is taking a pre-calculus class and she works for 3 hours each day on her homework. If she completed 90 problems in 6 days, how many problems can Heidi complete in 1 hour?

A. $\frac{1}{2}$

C. 15

B. 5

D. 30

6.RP.2

4. Dish detergent is $2.75 for 21 ounces. What is its unit rate?

A. $0.07/ounce
B. $0.08/ounce
C. $0.10/ounce
D. $0.13/ounce

6.RP.2

2. Harvey does sit-ups for 10 minutes each day. If he is able to complete 6,110 sit-ups in 13 days, how many sit-ups could Harvey do in 1 HOUR?

A. 470
B. 1,410
C. 2,115
D. 2,820

6.RP.2

5. Hannah uses 9 gallons of gas per day. If she drove for 16 days and went 2,592 miles, how many miles is she able to go on 1 gallon of gas?

A. 15 miles
B. 18 miles
C. 20 miles
D. 24 miles

6.RP.2

3. Ira purchased 8 packages of meat for $93.36. Each package was 3 pounds. How much would Ira pay for 1 pound of meat?

A. $3.89
B. $11.67
C. $21.40
D. $31.12

6.RP.2

6. The maximum weight for the ride was 375 pounds. Which inequality shows the weight, *w*, it can hold?

A. $w > 375$
B. $w < 375$
C. $w \geq 375$
D. $w \leq 375$

6.EE.8

When comparing prices of 2 items, it is better to find the unit rate of each package rather than just looking at the overall cost of a package.

1. Jonny could wash 120 cars in 8 hours. At that rate, how many cars could Jonny wash in 15 hours?

   A. 218
   B. 222
   C. 225
   D. 230

6.RP.3

3. Which beverage has the highest per ounce cost?

   A. Totally Tea
   B. Puncheriffic
   C. Ginger Beer
   D. The Caffinator

6.RP.3

Below is a table showing the cost and sizes of some soft drinks. **Use this information to answer questions 2 – 5.**

Drink	Ounces	Price
Totally Tea	64	$7.68
Puncheriffic	20	$1.80
Ginger Beer	32	$6.72
The Caffinator	18	$3.42

4. Which 2 beverages are closest in price per ounce?

   A. Totally Tea & Puncheriffic
   B. Puncheriffic & The Caffinator
   C. Ginger Beer & Totally Tea
   D. The Caffinator & Ginger Beer

6.RP.3

2. Which beverage has the lowest per ounce cost?

   A. Totally Tea
   B. Puncheriffic
   C. Ginger Beer
   D. The Caffinator

6.RP.3

5. How much would you expect 12 ounces of Puncheriffic to cost?

   A. $0.96
   B. $1.08
   C. $1.20
   D. $1.32

6.RP.3

Unit rates may be per hour, per gallon, per second or per quart.

Below is a table showing 4 students and how many laps they could run in a particular period of time (in minutes). **Use this information to answer questions 1 – 3.**

Student	Laps	Time (minutes)
Heather	11	10
Iggy	12.5	25
Jerome	11.05	13
Kimmy	8.5	17

1. Which student had the fastest time per lap?

  A. Heather

  B. Iggy

  C. Jerome

  D. Kimmy

6.RP.3

2. Which 2 students had the same time per lap?

  A. Heather & Iggy

  B. Iggy & Kimmy

  C. Jerome & Heather

  D. Kimmy & Jerome

6.RP.3

3. How many laps would Jerome be able to complete in 24 minutes?

  A. 19.9

  B. 20.4

  C. 21.3

  D. 21.5

6.RP.3

4. Express *"the sum of four times x and y"* as an algebraic expression.

  A. $4x + y$

  B. $4(x + y)$

  C. $4x - y$

  D. $4(x - y)$

6.EE.2

5. What is the solution to this equation:

$4b = 18$?

  A. $b = \dfrac{2}{9}$

  B. $b = \dfrac{7}{9}$

  C. $b = \dfrac{9}{2}$

  D. $b = \dfrac{9}{7}$

6.EE.7

Once you find the unit rate, that information can be used to find additional amounts.

Jenny bought $6\frac{1}{2}$ dozen roses for $79.56. **Use this information to answer questions 1 – 2.**

1. How much did Jenny pay per dozen?

A. $6.12
B. $8.49
C. $10.36
D. $12.24

6.RP.2

2. If Jenny bought 18 roses, how much would it cost?

A. $12.24
B. $15.42
C. $18.36
D. $21.08

6.RP.2

3. A bucket of chicken has 12 pieces and costs $9.48. After 3 pm it was on sale for $0.10 off per piece. What was the sale price per piece of chicken?

A. $0.64
B. $0.69
C. $0.74
D. $0.79

6.RP.3

4. Kelvin drove 210 miles in 3 hours and then took a break. After the break he drove 11 miles an hour slower than before the break. How fast did Kelvin drive after the break?

A. 54 mph
B. 59 mph
C. 70 mph
D. 81 mph

6.RP.3

5. Which equation is represented in the data from the chart below?

x	y
4	8
2.5	5
3	6

A. $y = 2x$

B. $x = 2y$

C. $y = \frac{1}{4}x$

D. $x = \frac{1}{4}y$

6.EE.9

DAY 6
CHALLENGE
QUESTION

Karen drove 496 miles in 8 hours. She then increased her speed by 3 mph. If she travels at this new speed for 5 hours, how far will she travel?

6.RP.3

Got questions? If you do, then Week 13 is the right place for you! It is all about statistical questions and identifying what would be good questions to ask when looking for specific data.

You can find detailed video explanations to each problem in the book by visiting:
ArgoPrep.com

1. What is 16% of 300?

  A. 24
  B. 32
  C. 48
  D. 64

6.RP.3

2. 30 is what percent of 250?

  A. 10%
  B. 12%
  C. 17%
  D. 20%

6.RP.3

3. What is 110% of 118?

  A. 11.8
  B. 106.2
  C. 129.8
  D. 141.6

6.RP.3

4. 50 is what percent of 25?

  A. 50%
  B. 100%
  C. 150%
  D. 200%

6.RP.3

5. The coordinates of the vertices of a rectangle are A (4, 2), B (4, -1), C (-7, -1) and D (-7, -2). What are the dimensions of the rectangle?

  A. 2 units by 3 units
  B. 3 units by 11 units
  C. 5 units by 4 units
  D. 7 units by 2 units

6.NS.8

6. How many gallons of lemonade would 5 people get if they equally shared $\frac{3}{4}$ gallon of lemonade?

  A. $\frac{3}{20}$ gallon   **D.** $\frac{5}{3}$ gallon

  B. $\frac{3}{5}$ gallon

  C. $\frac{5}{4}$ gallon

6.NS.1

Usually the word "OF" in a math problem indicates multiplication.

80

1. What is 24% of 52?

    A. 11.78
    B. 12.48
    C. 13.0
    D. 13.18

6.RP.3

4. 12 is 15% of what number?

    A. 50
    B. 60
    C. 70
    D. 80

6.RP.3

2. What is 2000% of 4?

    A. 0.8
    B. 8
    C. 80
    D. 800

6.RP.3

5. How many thirds are in $4\frac{4}{6}$?

    A. 14
    B. 17
    C. 20
    D. 23

6.NS.1

3. 47 is what percent of 141?

    A. 30.0%
    B. 33.3%
    C. 36.7%
    D. 39.2%

6.RP.3

6. What is 2,403 ÷ 27?

    A. 75
    B. 78
    C. 84
    D. 89

6.NS.2

If you a number more than doubles, it will have increased by more than 100%

WEEK 13 · DAY 3

ARGOPREP.COM

1. It took Kiera 12 hours to complete a 5,000 word paper. At this rate, how long would it take Kiera to write a 9,000 word paper?

A. 21.6 hours
B. 41.6 hours
C. 59.8 hours
D. 75 hours

6.RP.3

2. Using the table below, what is the missing number?

x	y
3	7.5
4	?
5	12.5

A. 4.5
B. 7.5
C. 10
D. 13

6.RP.3

3. If there are 250 students and 46% of them choose to major in the liberal arts, how many of the students will major in liberal arts?

A. 92
B. 115
C. 156
D. 204

6.RP.3

4. Kurt can sell 11 insurance policies in 2 weeks. How many policies could he sell in 5 weeks?

A. 25
B. 27.5
C. 29.5
D. 31

6.RP.3

5. Jessica was $\frac{1}{2}$ as tall as Kip. If Kip had a height of K, what was Jessica's height?

A. $\frac{1}{2}K$

B. $2K$

C. $2 + K$

D. $2 - K$

6.EE.6

A statistical question is one in which there are several possible answers.

1. Which question below is a statistical question?

   A. How many pairs of jeans do you own?
   B. How many pairs of jeans were sold each day during November?
   C. How many pairs of jeans did Mom wash in the last load?
   D. How many pairs of jeans are on the shelf?

6.SP.1

2. Which question below is a statistical question?

   A. How many letters are in the English alphabet?
   B. How many letters were in the mailroom yesterday?
   C. How many letters are in the names of the 6th grade students?
   D. How many letters are in your name?

6.SP.1

3. Which question below is a statistical question?

   A. Do you own a dog?
   B. How many pets do you have?
   C. How many cats are owned by the staff of Hope High School?
   D. How many turtles are in the pond?

6.SP.1

4. Which question below is a statistical question?

   A. How many hot dogs did each student eat?
   B. How many hot dogs were bought for the picnic?
   C. How many hot dogs were grilled?
   D. How many hot dogs had ketchup on them?

6.SP.1

5. What is the least common multiple of 12 and 9?

   A. 3
   B. 18
   C. 24
   D. 36

6.NS.4

6. There are 36 students and 20 of them are boys. What is the ratio of boys to girls?

   A. 4:5
   B. 5:4
   C. 5:9
   D. 9:5

6.RP.1

A Yes or No question is not a statistical question.

1. Daryl biked for 12 minutes and traveled 1.6 miles. If he kept the same pace, how far would he travel in 3.5 hours?

- **A.** 19.0 miles
- **B.** 22.4 miles
- **C.** 26.25 miles
- **D.** 28.0 miles

6.RP.3

2. Using the table below, what is the missing number?

x	y
7	1.75
?	1
2	0.5

- **A.** 3
- **B.** 4
- **C.** 5
- **D.** 6

6.RP.3

3. 14.28 is what percent of 119?

- **A.** 12%
- **B.** 14%
- **C.** 15%
- **D.** 17%

6.RP.3

4. Which question below is a statistical question?

- **A.** How many gumballs do you have?
- **B.** How many gumballs did Kent eat?
- **C.** How many red gumballs are in the 12 machines at the park?
- **D.** How much does a bag of gumballs cost?

6.SP.1

5. What is 0.8% of 264?

- **A.** 0.2112
- **B.** 2.112
- **C.** 21.12
- **D.** 211.2

6.RP.3

6. What is the coefficient of $7a^2b$?

- **A.** a
- **B.** b
- **C.** 2
- **D.** 7

6.EE.2

DAY 6
CHALLENGE QUESTION

Write a statistical question.

6.SP.1

WEEK 14

ARGOPREP.COM

VIDEO EXPLANATIONS

This week starts the beginning of a detailed study of data. You will begin to see how numbers in a data set relate to the set as a whole.

You can find detailed video explanations to each problem in the book by visiting:
ArgoPrep.com

Leslie kept track of her test scores and they are shown below. **Use this information to answer questions 1 – 3.** Round your answer to the nearest hundredth.

Test scores:	80	92	77	83	72	91	84

1. What is the median of the data?

- **A.** 4.0
- **B.** 20.0
- **C.** 82.7
- **D.** 83.0

6.SP.2

2. What is the range of the data?

- **A.** 4
- **B.** 20
- **C.** 22
- **D.** 23

6.SP.2

3. What is the mean of the data?

- **A.** 81.7
- **B.** 82.2
- **C.** 82.7
- **D.** 83.0

6.SP.2

Below is the data that was recorded about snowfall on certain days. It is measured in inches. **Use this information to answer questions 4 – 6.**

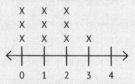

Snowfall (in inches)

4. Which amount of snowfall is this area LEAST likely to receive?

- **A.** 1 inch
- **B.** 2 inches
- **C.** 3 inches
- **D.** 4 inches

6.SP.2

5. What is the mean of the data?

- **A.** 0.7
- **B.** 1.0
- **C.** 1.2
- **D.** 1.5

6.SP.2

6. What is the range of the data set?

- **A.** 1
- **B.** 2
- **C.** 3
- **D.** 4

6.SP.2

The median is the middle number when all the data are in order from smallest to largest.

Matthew's coach kept record of the times that Matthew had when he ran his race at track meets. The data is shown below. All of the times are in minutes. **Use the given information to answer questions 1 – 3.**

Race #	Time	Race #	Time
1	25	6	22
2	24	7	19
3	23	8	21
4	23	9	20
5	24	10	19

1. What is the range of Matthew's race times?

- **A.** 6
- **B.** 8
- **C.** 19
- **D.** 25

6.SP.2

2. What is the median of the data set? Round your answer to the nearest tenth.

- **A.** 21.8
- **B.** 22.0
- **C.** 22.3
- **D.** 22.5

6.SP.2

3. What is the mean of the data? Round your answer to the nearest tenth.

- **A.** 21.8
- **B.** 22.0
- **C.** 22.3
- **D.** 22.5

6.SP.2

4. You can buy peanuts in bulk for $2.72 per pound. How much are the peanuts per ounce? Round your answer to the nearest cent.

- **A.** $0.13
- **B.** $0.15
- **C.** $0.17
- **D.** $0.20

6.RP.2

5. Which two expressions are equivalent for any value of k?

- **A.** $k \times k \times k$ and $3k$
- **B.** $5(2k - 4)$ and $10k - 4$
- **C.** $k + 3 + k + k + 7 + k$ and $2(2k + 5)$
- **D.** $3k + 8k - 2k$ and $10k$

6.EE.4

If there are 2 median numbers, those 2 numbers can be averaged to find the median of the data set.

Kia owns a restaurant and she records how much each table spends. The results are below and are given in dollars. **Use the given information to answer questions 1 – 4.**

Table 1	56	Table 5	87
Table 2	108	Table 6	72
Table 3	75	Table 7	69
Table 4	22	Table 8	90

1. What is the range of the data set?

   A. 22
   B. 76
   C. 86
   D. 108

6.SP.2

2. What is the median of the data set? Round your answer to the nearest tenth.

   A. 72.0
   B. 73.5
   C. 74.5
   D. 75.0

6.SP.2

3. What is the mean of the data? Round your answer to the nearest tenth.

   A. 64.3
   B. 69.5
   C. 72.4
   D. 82.7

6.SP.2

4. Which number gives the most accurate picture of the data set?

   A. mean
   B. median
   C. mode
   D. range

6.SP.2

5. Kezia bought 5 books for $21. Which equation shows the relationship between the number of books, b, and C, the total cost for the books?

   A. $C = 4.2b$
   B. $4.2C = b$
   C. $5C = 21b$
   D. $21C = 5b$

6.EE.9

The range is the difference between the largest and the smallest numbers in a data set.

Below shows the scores for a particular art class. **Use this information to answer questions 1 – 4.**

Spanish Score						
7	2	7	8			
8	2	2	4	5	7	7	8
9	1	2	3	3	7	
10	0					

3. What is the mean of the data, rounded to the nearest tenth?

A. 86.8
B. 87.3
C. 87.6
D. 88.1

6.SP.2

1. What is the range of the data set?

A. 3
B. 18
C. 28
D. 33

6.SP.2

4. Which number is NOT one of the modes?

A. 82
B. 87
C. 92
D. 93

6.SP.2

2. What is the median of the data set?

A. 85
B. 87
C. 88
D. 90

6.SP.2

5. The rope was 256 feet long. If each piece of rope was cut so that it was 12 feet long, how many 12-foot pieces could be made from the rope?

A. 21
B. 22
C. 24
D. 25

6.NS.2

Mean is another way to say average. It can be found by adding all of a set of numbers together and then dividing by however many numbers were added.

The number of quarters that some children had is listed below. **Use this information to answer questions 1 – 3.**

Quarters:	42	55	8	45	51	49	50	47

1. What is the range of the data set?

- **A.** 8
- **B.** 36
- **C.** 42
- **D.** 47

6.SP.2

2. What is the median of the data set? Round your answer to the nearest tenth.

- **A.** 47
- **B.** 48
- **C.** 49
- **D.** 50

6.SP.2

3. What is the mean of the data?

- **A.** 42.8
- **B.** 43.4
- **C.** 44.1
- **D.** 44.7

6.SP.2

4. Which number gives the most accurate picture of the data set?

- **A.** mean
- **B.** median
- **C.** mode
- **D.** range

6.SP.2

5. Which equation is represented in the data from the chart below?

x	y
13.5	4.5
3.9	1.3
7.2	2.4

- **A.** $y = 9x$
- **B.** $x = 9y$
- **C.** $y = \frac{1}{3}x$
- **D.** $x = \frac{1}{3}y$

6.EE.9

DAY 6

CHALLENGE QUESTION

Using the data from questions 1 – 4, if the 8 was removed from the data set, what would be the new mean? Round your answer to the nearest tenth.

6.SP.2

WEEK 15

ARGOPREP.COM

VIDEO EXPLANATIONS

You will have plenty of opportunities to find numbers that summarize and help to describe given sets of data. Week 15 focuses on measures of center.

You can find detailed video explanations to each problem in the book by visiting:
ArgoPrep.com

The temperatures for Springfield, Ohio were recorded for the month of August. The results are below. **Use this data to answer questions 1 – 3.**

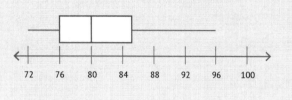

1. What is the inter-quartile range (IQR) for the data set shown?

A. 4
B. 5
C. 9
D. 12

6.SP.3

2. What is the range for the data set shown?

A. 4
B. 11
C. 18
D. 24

6.SP.3

3. What is the median of the data set?

A. 72
B. 76
C. 80
D. 85

6.SP.3

4. 13 is what percent of 65?

A. 10%
B. 20%
C. 25%
D. 33%

6.RP.3

5. Christine had a balance of - $263.95 at the beginning of the day. By the end of the day her balance was zero. Which statement best describes what happened?

A. Christine spent $263.95.
B. Christine borrowed $263.95.
C. Christine deposited $263.95.
D. Christine withdrew $263.95.

6.NS.5

6. The coordinates of the vertices of a rectangle are A (-8, 1), B (2, 1), C (2, -5) and D (-8, -5). What are the dimensions of the rectangle?

A. 1 units by 16 units
B. 3 units by 6 units
C. 4 units by 3 units
D. 6 units by 10 units

6.NS.8

In a box plot, the median can be found where the 2nd quartile ends and the 3rd quartile begins.

The scores for Jasmine's English class are shown below. **Use the given information to answer questions 1 – 4.**

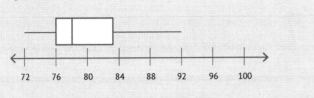

72 76 80 84 88 92 96 100

1. What is the median of the data set?

  A. 72
  B. 78
  C. 83
  D. 92

6.SP.3

2. What is the inter-quartile range (IQR) for the data set shown?

  A. 2
  B. 5
  C. 7
  D. 10

6.SP.3

3. What is the range for the data set shown?

  A. 4
  B. 7
  C. 15
  D. 20

6.SP.3

4. Which statement is true about the data set provided?

  A. The median is larger than the range.
  B. The data set has a range of 28.
  C. The largest number in the set is 100.
  D. The minimum value of the set is 76.

6.SP.3

5. Which of the following is a statistical question?

  A. What are the ages of the students in your class?
  B. How old are you?
  C. Who is the oldest person in your class?
  D. Are you 13 years old?

6.SP.1

6. What is the value of the expression below?

$$2 + 6^3 - (7^2 - 4)$$

  A. 165
  B. 173
  C. 459
  D. 467

6.EE.1

A measure of center can be used to summarize a data set.

The distances that Luca walked are shown below in kilometers. **Arrange the data into a box plot to answer questions 1 – 5.**

Luca walked:	15	22	19	15	23	18	20

1. What is the range for the data set shown?

A. 6
B. 8
C. 10
D. 12

6.SP.3

2. What is the median of the data set?

A. 15
B. 18
C. 19
D. 22

6.SP.3

3. What is the inter-quartile range (IQR) for the data set shown?

A. 7
B. 8
C. 9
D. 10

6.SP.3

4. What integer is closest to the mean of the data set?

A. 15
B. 17
C. 19
D. 21

6.SP.2

5. Which statement is true about the data set provided?

A. There is no mode.
B. The IQR and range are the same.
C. The mean is less than the median.
D. The mode is in the third quartile.

6.SP.3

6. If there are 310 teachers and 25% of them work a second job, how many of the teachers work a second job? Round answer to the nearest whole number.

A. 72
B. 75
C. 78
D. 83

6.RP.3

Range helps determine the amount of variance in a data set.

The heights for several students in Ms. O'Hara's 4th grade class were recorded. **The results were in inches and they are shown below. Use this data to answer questions 1 – 4.**

Height (in)

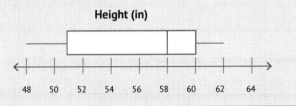

48 50 52 54 56 58 60 62 64

1. What is the inter-quartile range (IQR) for the data set shown?

A. 2
B. 7
C. 9
D. 12

6.SP.3

2. What is the range for the data set shown?

A. 7
B. 9
C. 14
D. 16

6.SP.3

3. What is the median of the data set?

A. 51
B. 58
C. 60
D. 64

6.SP.3

4. Which statement is true about the data set?

A. About half of the students are taller than 58 inches.
B. The shortest student is 47 inches.
C. The tallest student is 64 inches.
D. About half of the students are between 48 – 62 inches tall.

6.SP.3

Use the rectangular coordinate system and the parallelogram shown below to answer question 5.

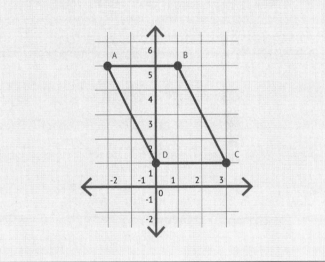

5. What is the distance of Line Segment CD?

A. 1 unit   C. 3 units
B. 2 units   D. 4 units

6.NS.8

When considering box plots, be sure to read the labels on the number line.

95

Mr. Dorman's class kept record of how many ornaments were on each student's Christmas trees at home. **The results are shown below. Use the given information to answer questions 1 – 4.**

Ornaments					
0	7	8			
1	2	2	5	7	8
2	1	3	3	7	
3	0				

1. What is the range of the data set?

A. 6
B. 7
C. 18
D. 23

6.SP.3

2. What is the mean for the data set shown (rounded to the tenths)?

A. 16.9
B. 17.8
C. 18.3
D. 18.6

6.SP.3

3. What is the median of the data set?

A. 15.5   **D.** 18.5
B. 16.5
C. 17.5

6.SP.3

4. Which statement is true about the data set?

A. Some students had 0 ornaments.
B. No one had more than 18 ornaments.
C. Two students had 17 ornaments.
D. The most ornaments a student had was 30.

6.SP.3

5. There are 48 cars and 12 of them are blue. What is the ratio of blue cars to cars?

A. 1:2   **D.** 1:5
B. 1:3
C. 1:4

6.RP.1

6. 300 is what percent of 200?

A. 66.7%   **C.** 150%
B. 100%   **D.** 166.7%

6.RP.3

DAY 6
CHALLENGE QUESTION

Using the data set from #'s 1 – 4 shown above, if all of the students in Mr. Dorman's answered the survey about ornaments, how many students does Mr. Dorman have in his class?

6.SP.5

96

WEEK 16

ARGOPREP.COM

VIDEO EXPLANATIONS

In Week 16 you will have the chance to zoom in on data sets so you can see how each piece of data combines with the other data points to form one large plot that represents the whole data set.

You can find detailed video explanations to each problem in the book by visiting:
ArgoPrep.com

WEEK 16 · DAY 1

Use the tables below to answer questions 1 – 4.

Table A

2	3	2
5	1	6
4	7	1
2	3	6
1	2	2

Table B

6	7	4
2	4	3
3	5	2
7	2	3
4	4	7

Table C

6	5	2
3	6	4
1	5	3
5	4	3
4	2	6

Table D

4	3	6
3	7	4
2	4	5
6	4	5
4	6	3

3. Which data set is shown below?

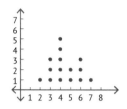

- **A.** Table A
- **B.** Table B
- **C.** Table C
- **D.** Table D

6.SP.4

4. Which data set is shown below?

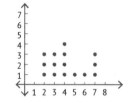

- **A.** Table A
- **B.** Table B
- **C.** Table C
- **D.** Table D

6.SP.4

1. Which data set is shown below?

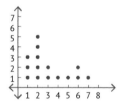

- **A.** Table A
- **B.** Table B
- **C.** Table C
- **D.** Table D

6.SP.4

2. Which data set is shown below?

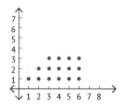

- **A.** Table A
- **B.** Table B
- **C.** Table C
- **D.** Table D

6.SP.4

5. Which data set is shown below?

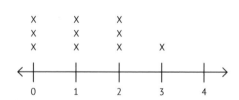

- **A.** 0, 2, 1, 1, 4, 3, 2, 0, 2, 2
- **B.** 1, 0, 3, 2, 1, 2, 3, 0, 2, 2
- **C.** 3, 3, 2, 1, 0, 3, 1, 2, 3, 0
- **D.** 1, 0, 0, 2, 3, 1, 1, 2, 0, 2

6.SP.4

When plotting data, there should be one plot for each piece of data in the set.

Use the four tables shown below to answer questions 1 – 4.

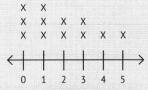

Graph A

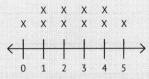

Graph B

Graph C

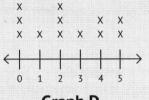

Graph D

3. Which graph shows the data below?

2, 3, 4, 4, 0, 2, 1, 1, 3, 5, 3, 2

A. Graph A **D.** Graph D
B. Graph B
C. Graph C

6.SP.4

4. Which graph shows the data below?

1, 4, 3, 2, 0, 0, 1, 4, 2, 4, 5, 0

A. Graph A **D.** Graph D
B. Graph B
C. Graph C

6.SP.4

1. Which graph above shows the data below?

0, 5, 4, 4, 2, 3, 2, 1, 0, 0, 2, 5

A. Graph A **C.** Graph C
B. Graph B **D.** Graph D

6.SP.4

2. Which graph above shows the data below?

0, 2, 3, 4, 1, 0, 2, 5, 1, 1, 3, 0

A. Graph A **C.** Graph C
B. Graph B **D.** Graph D

6.SP.4

5. Using the table below, what is the missing number?

x	y
?	$\frac{5}{2}$
8	4
14	7

A. 4
B. 5
C. 6
D. 7

6.RP.3

Data can be shown in a variety of ways. Information can be plotted on graphs, dot plots, box plots and other methods.

WEEK 16 · DAY 3

Below are 4 tables that record the number of major storms during 10 year periods of time. **Use the 4 data sets below to answer questions 1 – 4.**

Table A

Time Period	Storms
1970 - 1979	卌 |||
1980 - 1989	卌 卌 卌	
1990 - 1999	卌 卌
2000 - 2009	卌 卌 ||||
2010 - 2020	||||

Table B

Time Period	Storms
1970 - 1979	卌 |||
1980 - 1989	卌 卌 ||
1990 - 1999	卌 卌
2000 - 2009	卌 |||
2010 - 2020	卌	

Table C

Time Period	Storms
1970 - 1979	卌 卌 ||
1980 - 1989	|||
1990 - 1999	卌 |||
2000 - 2009	卌 ||||
2010 - 2020	卌 卌

Table D

Time Period	Storms
1970 - 1979	卌 |||
1980 - 1989	卌
1990 - 1999	卌	
2000 - 2009	卌 |||
2010 - 2020	卌 卌	

1. Which data set is graphed below?

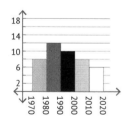

- **A.** Table A
- **B.** Table B
- **C.** Table C
- **D.** Table D

6.SP.4

2. Which data set is graphed below?

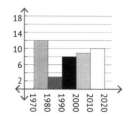

- **A.** Table A
- **B.** Table B
- **C.** Table C
- **D.** Table D

6.SP.4

3. Which data set is graphed below?

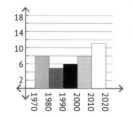

- **A.** Table A
- **B.** Table B
- **C.** Table C
- **D.** Table D

6.SP.4

4. Which data set is graphed below?

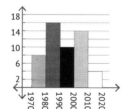

- **A.** Table A
- **B.** Table B
- **C.** Table C
- **D.** Table D

6.SP.4

5. Lu bought 8 cookies for $6. Which equation shows the relationship between the number of cookies, n, and C, the total cost for the cookies?

- **A.** $C = 0.75n$
- **C.** $6C = 8n$
- **B.** $0.75C = n$
- **D.** $8C = 6n$

6.EE.9

Histograms are useful to show periods of time or numbers.

Below are four tables showing the number of times students asked to borrow a pencil on 12 different days. **Use the tables below to answer questions 1 – 4.**

Table A

2	7	4	2
4	3	2	6
1	4	6	4

Table B

8	2	2	4
4	1	4	6
2	7	2	7

Table C

1	2	6	4
3	4	1	2
2	7	1	6

Table D

8	2	1	2
5	7	6	8
2	3	8	5

1. Which data set is graphed below?

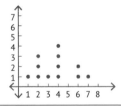

- **A.** Table A
- **B.** Table B
- **C.** Table C
- **D.** Table D

6.SP.4

2. Which data set is graphed below?

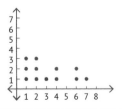

- **A.** Table A
- **B.** Table B
- **C.** Table C
- **D.** Table D

6.SP.4

3. Which data set is graphed below?

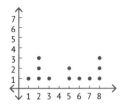

- **A.** Table A
- **B.** Table B
- **C.** Table C
- **D.** Table D

6.SP.4

4. Which data set is graphed below?

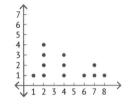

- **A.** Table A
- **B.** Table B
- **C.** Table C
- **D.** Table D

6.SP.4

5. Bethel made bagels and could package 13 of them in each box. If she made 4,012 bagels, how many full boxes would she have?

- **A.** 38
- **B.** 298
- **C.** 308
- **D.** 309

6.NS.2

When graphing data, make sure to count the pieces of data to make sure each piece is present in the graph or plot.

Four different students surveyed random strangers about the amount of money that they had in their pockets. The students recorded the information in different ways and the plots of their surveys are shown below. **Use these graphs to answer questions 1 – 4.**

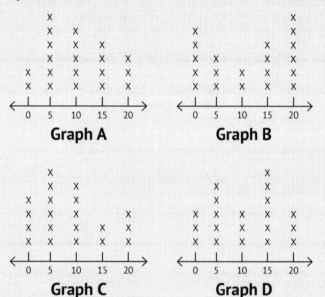

Graph A

Graph B

Graph C

Graph D

1. Which graph shows the data set below?

Money Amount	People
0	IIII
5	IIII I
10	IIII
15	II
20	III

A. Graph A
B. Graph B
C. Graph C
D. Graph D

6.SP.4

2. Which graph shows the data set below?

Data Set: 0, 5, 10 5, 5, 20, 5, 10, 15, 15, 5, 10, 0, 5, 10, 15, 10, 20, 15, 20

A. Graph A   C. Graph C
B. Graph B   D. Graph D

6.SP.4

3. Which graph shows the data set below?

0	10	20	15	15
20	5	15	5	0
15	20	0	0	20
10	0	20	20	5

A. Graph A   C. Graph C
B. Graph B   D. Graph D

6.SP.4

4. Which graph shows the data set below?

Data Set: 0, 5, 10, 5, 5, 20, 5, 20, 5, 15, 0, 15, 10, 15, 10, 15, 15, 0, 20, 15

A. Graph A   C. Graph C
B. Graph B   D. Graph D

6.SP.4

5. What is the mean of Graph A from above?

A. 5   C. 15
B. 10   D. 20

6.SP.3

DAY 6

CHALLENGE QUESTION

Create a dot plot using the following data set:

1	4	3
3	1	3
2	5	2

6.SP.4

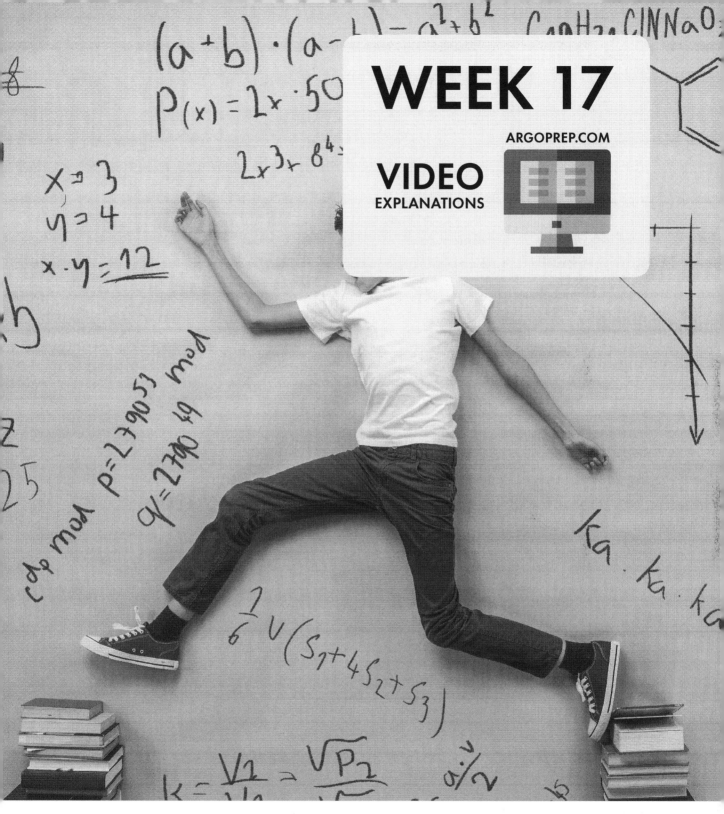

This week you can begin to see what each data piece represents. How many observations were there?
How was the data measured? What is the mean or median of the data set?

**You can find detailed video explanations to each problem in the book by visiting:
ArgoPrep.com**

The chart below shows the distance 4 students ran in 27 minutes. **Use the table below to answer questions 1 – 4.**

Student	Distance
Khalid	4,696 meters
Lars	5 kilometers
Marcy	5,307 meters
Deena	4.7 kilometers

1. Which student ran the farthest?

A. Khalid
B. Lars
C. Marcy
D. Deena

6.SP.5

2. Which student ran the shortest distance?

A. Khalid
B. Lars
C. Marcy
D. Deena

6.SP.5

3. Which 2 students ran almost the same distance?

A. Khalid & Deena
B. Lars & Marcy
C. Marcy & Khalid
D. Deena & Lars

6.SP.5

4. Lyla has $12 more than Melanie. If Lyla has L dollars, how many dollars does Melanie have?

A. $12L$ C. $L + 12$
B. $12 - L$ D. $L - 12$

6.EE.6

5. Which value(s) of Set s are true for the equation $-5s \geq 10$?

$s = \{-3, -2, 0, 1, 2, 5\}$

A. $0, 1, 2, 5$
B. -3
C. $-3, -2$
D. $-2, 0, 1, 2, 5$

6.EE.5

6. What is 18.5% of 4000? 6.RP.3

A. 7.4   C. 740
B. 74   D. 7,400

6.RP.3

TIP **of the DAY**

When looking at data sets, be sure to read the labels and units.

The dot plot below shows how many pets each student in Ms. Peeler's class has. **Use the information to answer questions 1 – 5.**

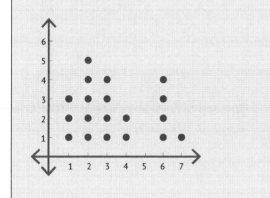

3. How many students are in Ms. Peeler's class?

A. 7   **D.** 20
B. 17
C. 19

6.SP.5

4. How many students have 1 pet?

A. 1   **D.** 7
B. 3
C. 6

6.SP.5

1. What is the largest number of pets any one student has?

A. 2
B. 5
C. 6
D. 7

6.SP.5

5. What is the TOTAL number of pets owned by all the students in Ms. Peeler's class?

A. 19   **D.** 64
B. 35
C. 56

6.SP.5

2. What number of pets do most students have?

A. 2
B. 3
C. 6
D. 7

6.SP.5

6. The width of a runner is 6 1/4 feet. If the area of the runner is 93 3/4 square feet, what is the length of the runner?

A. 13 feet   **D.** 18 feet
B. 15 feet
C. 16 feet

6.NS.1

Read carefully to see if a dot or other plot point represents ONE item or a PAIR or MANY (such as 5 or 10).

Below is a graph showing the colors of cars in the parking lot. **Use this information to answer questions 1 – 6.**

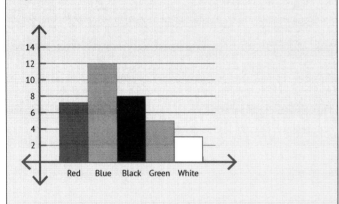

1. Which color has the most cars in the parking lot?

A. red
B. blue
C. black
D. green

6.SP.5

2. How many cars are in the parking lot?

A. 12
B. 25
C. 32
D. 35

6.SP.5

3. How many white cars are in the parking lot?

A. 3
B. 5
C. 7
D. 8

6.SP.5

4. How many blue OR black cars are there in the lot?

A. 8
B. 12
C. 17
D. 20

6.SP.5

5. What is the ratio of red cars to green cars?

A. 5:7
B. 8:5
C. 7:5
D. 12:7

6.RP.1

6. What is the ratio of green cars to cars?

A. 1:5
B. 1:7
C. 5:1
D. 7:1

6.RP.1

You are doing great! You have completed over 16 weeks worth of work – keep it up!

106

Each student in third period was asked how many pairs of shoes they had. The results are below. **Use this information to answer questions 1 – 6.**

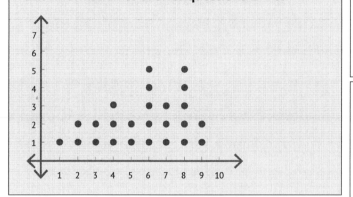

1. What is the largest number of shoes that EVERY student has?

A. 1   **C.** 6
B. 5   **D.** 8

6.SP.5

2. Which statements is true about the above data set?

A. The most shoes any one student has is 8 pairs of shoes.
B. There are 6 students who have 5 pairs of shoes.
C. There are 26 students in third period.
D. More than half of the students have more than 5 pairs of shoes.

6.SP.5

3. How many students are in third period?

A. 20
B. 23
C. 25
D. 26

6.SP.5

4. How many pairs of shoes are owned in TOTAL by all of the students in third period?

A. 138
B. 142
C. 153
D. 157

6.SP.5

5. What is the mean number of the data (rounded to the nearest tenth)?

A. 4.8
B. 5.7
C. 6.0
D. 7.1

6.SP.3

6. What is the median number of the data?

A. 6
B. 7
C. 8
D. 9

6.SP.3

When you take tomorrow's assessment, be sure to read the labels and units for any graphs and/or tables.

Students' activities were measured and the number of minutes per activity per day is shown below.. **Use this information to answer questions 1 – 6.**

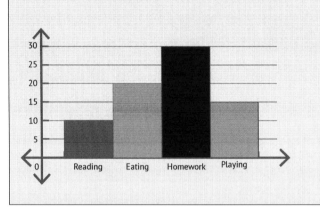

3. How many minutes PER WEEK did students spend playing?

A. 15   **D.** 105

B. 21

C. 75

6.SP.5

4. Which activity did students spend 20 minutes on?

A. reading   **D.** playing

B. eating

C. homework

6.SP.5

1. Which activity did students spend the most time on?

A. reading

B. eating

C. homework

D. playing

6.SP.5

5. What is the ratio between time spent playing and time spent eating?

A. 1:2

B. 2:3

C. 3:4

D. 4:3

6.RP.1

2. Which activity did students spend the least amount of time on?

A. reading

B. eating

C. homework

D. playing

6.SP.5

6. What is the ratio between time spent doing homework and time spent doing something else?

A. 1:2   **D.** 4:3

B. 2:3

C. 3:4

6.RP.1

DAY 6
CHALLENGE
QUESTION

Using the table from above, what is the total number of minutes recorded in the graph?

6.SP.5

If you ever need to buy carpet for a room or plant grass in your backyard, you will need to know how to find the area of the carpet and grass. Week 18 gives you lots of practice finding the area of figures.

You can find detailed video explanations to each problem in the book by visiting:
ArgoPrep.com

WEEK 18 · DAY 1

---

1. What is the area of the figure below?

11 feet

11 feet

A. 22 square feet
B. 44 square feet
C. 121 square feet
D. 14,641 square feet

6.G.1

---

2. The octagon below is made of 8 triangles that each have a base of 3 cm and a height of 2 cm. What is the area of the octagon?

A. 24 cm²
B. 48 cm²
C. 96 cm²
D. 192 cm²

6.G.1

---

3. What is the area of the figure below?

9 inches

12 inches

A. 21 inches²
B. 32 inches²
C. 54 inches²
D. 108 inches²

6.G.1

---

4. The trapezoid below has been sectioned into a square and a triangle. What is its area?

9 inches

5 inches

A. 22.5 in²
B. 35 in²
C. 45 in²
D. 47.5 in²

6.G.1

---

5. The pool pump uses 1,680 units of electricity over 2 weeks. It ran 5 hours per day. How much energy was used per hour?

A. 24 units
B. 34 units
C. 106 units
D. 168 units

6.RP.2

---

6. What is the greatest common factor of 49 and 63?

A. 1
B. 3
C. 7
D. 19

6.NS.4

TIP of the DAY

When finding the area of a triangle or a trapezoid, remember to divide by 2.

1. What is the area of the figure below?

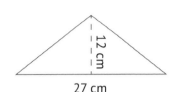

12 cm

27 cm

A. 39 cm²
B. 115 cm²
C. 162 cm²
D. 324 cm²

6.G.1

2. What is the area of the figure below?

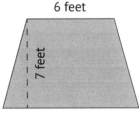

6 feet

7 feet

9 feet

A. 51 ft²
B. 52.5 ft²
C. 61 ft²
D. 378 ft²

6.G.1

The shape below contains a square, a right triangle and 2 rectangles. **Use the information given to answer questions 3 – 6.**

NOTE: Figure not drawn to scale.

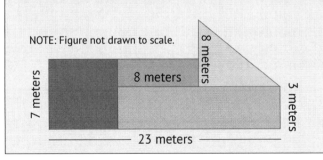

7 meters

8 meters

8 meters

3 meters

23 meters

3. What is the area of the larger rectangle?

A. 24 m²
B. 32 m²
C. 48 m²
D. 69 m²

6.G.1

4. What is the area of the smaller rectangle?

A. 24 m²
B. 32 m²
C. 48 m²
D. 69 m²

6.G.1

5. What is the area of the triangle?

A. 24 m²
B. 32 m²
C. 48 m²
D. 64 m²

6.G.1

6. What is the total area for the entire figure?

A. 161 m²
B. 177 m²
C. 185 m²
D. 193 m²

6.G.1

Area is measured in square units (i.e. ft² or m²).

1. What is the area of the shape below?

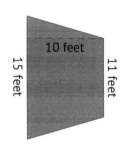

10 feet

15 feet

11 feet

A. 46 ft²
B. 130 ft²
C. 157.5 ft²
D. 260 ft²

6.G.1

4. What is the area of the figure below?

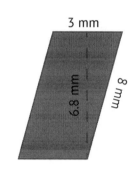

3 mm

6.8 mm

8 mm

A. 12.0 mm²
B. 16.2 mm²
C. 17.8 mm²
D. 20.4 mm²

6.G.1

2. A square has a side length of 27 millimeters. What is the area of the square?

A. 108 mm²
B. 729 mm²
C. 1,024 mm²
D. 2,017 mm²

6.G.1

5. What is the least common multiple of 11 and 4?

A. 1
B. 11
C. 22
D. 44

6.NS.4

3. What is the area of the figure below?

6 centimeters

46 centimeters

A. 52 cm²
B. 104 cm²
C. 203 cm²
D. 276 cm²

6.G.1

6. In order to have a healthy heart it is recommended that your cholesterol not be more than 200. Which inequality shows the "healthy" amount of c, cholesterol?

A. $c > 200$
B. $c \geq 200$
C. $c < 200$
D. $c \leq 200$

6.EE.8

 **TIP** of the **DAY**

When finding the area of a square, you need to multiply the side lengths, so the formula for the area of a square is $A = s^2$.

WEEK 18 · DAY 4

1. What is the area of the figure below?

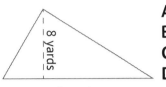

8 yards

9 yards

A. 17 yards²
B. 36 yards²
C. 72 yards²
D. 144 yards²

6.G.1

2. The figure below has 2 triangles that are exactly the same. These triangles have 2 legs that are both 5 units long. The third part of the figure is a square. What is the area of the figure below?

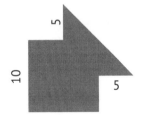

5

10

5

A. 62.5 units²
B. 75 units²
C. 112.5 units²
D. 125 units²

6.G.1

3. What is the area of the figure below?

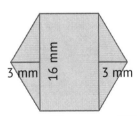

3 mm   16 mm   3 mm

15 mm

NOTE: Figure drawn not to scale.

A. 144 mm²
B. 264 mm²
C. 288 mm²
D. 336 mm²

6.G.1

4. There is a regular octagon that is composed of 8 triangles. If one of the triangles has a base of 8 centimeters and a height of 11 centimeters, what is the total area of the octagon?

A. 176 cm²
B. 352 cm²
C. 514 cm²
D. 704 cm²

6.G.1

5. What is the solution to this equation:

$$d - 3\frac{1}{5} = 7\frac{1}{4}?$$

A. $d = 4\frac{1}{20}$

B. $d = 4\frac{1}{5}$

C. $d = 10\frac{9}{20}$

D. $d = 10\frac{4}{5}$

6.EE.7

6. What is the largest integer value for x that would make $13x < -39$ true?

A. – 6
B. – 4
C. 0
D. 5

6.EE.5

The height of a triangle is not always one of its sides.

1. What is the area of the hexagon shown that has 6 equilateral triangles?

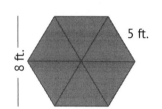

5 ft.

8 ft.

A. 20 ft²
B. 30 ft²
C. 40 ft²
D. 60 ft²

NOTE: Figure not drawn to scale.

6.G.1

Use the composite figure below to answer questions 2 – 5. It was measured in meters.

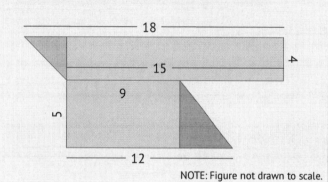

18

4

15

9

5

12

NOTE: Figure not drawn to scale.

2. What is the area of the longest rectangle?

A. 36 m²
B. 38 m²
C. 60 m²
D. 72 m²

6.G.1

3. What is the area of the 2 triangles combined?

A. 12 m²   **C.** 14.5 m²
B. 13.5 m²   **D.** 15 m²

6.G.1

4. What is the area of the shorter rectangle?

A. 30 m²   **C.** 60 m²
B. 45 m²   **D.** 108 m²

6.G.1

5. What is the area of the entire figure combined?

A. 118.5 m²   **C.** 132.0 m²
B. 119.5 m²   **D.** 158.0 m²

6.G.1

6. A line segment is shown below. What are the endpoints' coordinates?

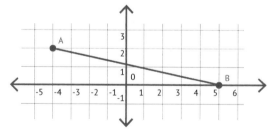

A. A (2, -4), B (0, 5)
B. A (-4, 2), B (0, 5)
C. A (2, -4), B (5, 0)
D. A (-4, 2), B (5, 0)

6.NS.8

DAY 6

CHALLENGE
QUESTION

Look at the composite figure used for questions 2 – 5. If the longer rectangle were removed, what would be the area of the remaining figure?

6.G.1

WEEK 19

ARGOPREP.COM

VIDEO EXPLANATIONS

In Week 19 you will be able to calculate the volume of three-dimensional objects – or determine the amount of space that that object occupies.

You can find detailed video explanations to each problem in the book by visiting: ArgoPrep.com

1. What is the volume of a rectangular prism that is 8 1/2 inches tall, 4 inches wide and 12 1/4 inches deep?

A. 96.0 in³

B. 406.72 in³

C. 408.0 in³

D. 416.5 in³

6.G.2

2. What is the volume of the tent below?

A. 157.5 ft³

B. 183.75 ft³

C. 257.25 ft³

D. 315.0 ft³

6.G.2

3. The rectangular prism below is made of cubes that have 1/3-inch sides. What is the volume of the prism?

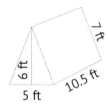

A. $\frac{8}{27}$ in³

C. $\frac{8}{9}$ in³

B. $\frac{16}{27}$ in³

D. $\frac{16}{9}$ in³

6.G.2

4. What is the volume of the rectangular prism below?

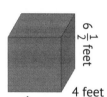

6 $\frac{1}{2}$ feet

4 feet

5 $\frac{1}{4}$ feet

A. 47.3 ft³

B. 68.3 ft³

C. 126.5 ft³

D. 136.5 ft³

6.G.2

5. How many liters of gas would 3 lawn mowers get if 7/8 - liter of gas was shared equally?

A. $\frac{7}{24}$ liter

D. $\frac{8}{10}$ liter

B. $\frac{8}{21}$ liter

C. $\frac{7}{11}$ liter

6.NS.1

6. What is 22.8% of 1200?

A. 268.4

B. 273.6

C. 285.9

D. 291.5

6.RP.3

Three dimensions are needed to find volume: length x width x height.

1. There is a right triangular prism that has a triangular base. The triangle has a base that is 8 1/2 meters with a 7 meter height. The prism is 11 1/4 meters long. What is the volume of this triangular prism? (Round to tenths.)

A. 80.3 m³   **C.** 334.7 m³
B. 428.6 m³   **D.** 669.4 m³

6.G.2

This rectangular prism is made up of unit squares. **Use this information to answer questions 2 – 3.**

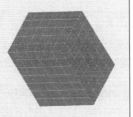

2. If each unit square is 1 in³, what is the volume of the prism?

A. 107 in³   **C.** 210 in³
B. 147 in³   **D.** 214 in³

6.G.2

3. If the above figure's unit cubes had sides that were 1/2 inch, then what would the volume of the prism be?

A. 26 1/4 in³   **C.** 73 1/2 in³
B. 53 1/2 in³   **D.** 105 in³

6.G.2

4. The figure below has a base that is 3/4 meter by 3/4 meter. What is the volume of the figure?

12 meters

A. $3\frac{3}{8}$ m³

B. $4\frac{7}{8}$ m³

C. $5\frac{1}{4}$ m³

D. $6\frac{3}{4}$ m³

6.G.2

5. What is 6908 ÷ 44?

A. 155
B. 157
C. 159
D. 161

6.NS.2

6. How many eighths are in $3\frac{3}{4}$?

A. 24
B. 30
C. 32
D. 36

6.NS.1

Volume is measured in cubic units (cm³, ft³, etc.).

1. The rectangular prism below is made of cubes that have 1/2-centimeter sides. What is the volume of the prism?

- **A.** 6 cm³
- **B.** 8 cm³
- **C.** 10 cm³
- **D.** 12 cm³

6.G.2

2. A rectangular prism has a base that is 5 1/3 inches wide and is 5 2/5 inches long. If the height is 9 inches, what is the prism's volume?

- **A.** $257\frac{3}{5}$ in³
- **C.** $260\frac{4}{5}$ in³
- **B.** $259\frac{1}{5}$ in³
- **D.** $262\frac{2}{5}$ in³

6.G.2

3. The rectangular prism below is made of cubes that have 3/4-inch sides. What is the volume of the prism?

- **A.** $2\frac{1}{2}$ in³
- **B.** $5\frac{1}{4}$ in³
- **C.** $8\frac{3}{4}$ in³
- **D.** $10\frac{1}{8}$ in³

6.G.2

4. What is the volume of the rectangular prism below?

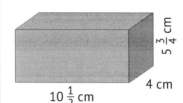

5 3/4 cm

4 cm

$10\frac{1}{2}$ cm

- **A.** $229\frac{1}{2}$ cm³
- **B.** $236\frac{1}{2}$ cm³
- **C.** $241\frac{1}{2}$ cm³
- **D.** $251\frac{1}{2}$ cm³

6.G.2

5. Which question below is a statistical question?

- **A.** How many pairs of shoes do 6th graders have?
- **B.** How many TVs are in Neveah's house?
- **C.** How far did Owen drive yesterday?
- **D.** Do you like ketchup?

6.SP.1

6. What is the median weight shown

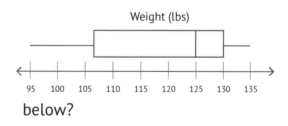

Weight (lbs)

95 100 105 110 115 120 125 130 135

below?

- **A.** 25
- **C.** 115
- **B.** 40
- **D.** 125

6.SP.3

TIP of the DAY

Volume = length x width x height.

1. What is the volume of the rectangular prism below? (Round to the tenths.)

$6\frac{1}{2}$ feet

$30\frac{1}{5}$ ft

A. 1276.0 ft³   **C.** 1318.4 ft³

B. 1288.6 ft³   **D.** 1346.9 ft³

6.G.2

Below are students at a primary school. **Use the information below to answer questions 4 - 6.**

Pre-kindergarten	20
Kindergarten	75
First Grade	48
Second Grade	51

2. There is a prism that is 6 3/4 cm tall. What is its volume if it is a right triangular prism that has a triangle with a base of 10 2/3 cm and a height of 7 cm?

A. 249.1 cm³   **C.** 255.2 cm³

B. 252.0 cm³   **D.** 258.6cm³

6.G.2

4. What is the ratio of kindergarten to pre-kindergarten students?

A. 4:5   **C.** 5:4

B. 4:15   **D.** 15:4

6.RP.1

3. The rectangular prism below is made of cubes that have 1/3-inch sides. What is the volume of the prism?

A. $1\frac{1}{9}$ in³

B. $1\frac{5}{27}$ in³

C. $2\frac{2}{27}$ in³

D. $3\frac{5}{9}$ in³

6.G.2

5. What is the ratio of first grade to second grade students?

A. 8:9   **C.** 16:17

B. 9:8   **D.** 17:16

6.RP.1

6. What is the ratio of pre-kindergarten to first grade students?

A. 12:5   **C.** 4:1

B. 5:12   **D.** 1:3

6.RP.1

Like area, volume can be cumulative, or added.

TIP of the DAY

1. What is the volume of the rectangular prism below? It is a perfect cube. Round your answer to the nearest tenth.

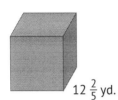

12 $\frac{2}{5}$ yd.

A. 334.8 yd³
B. 1254.1 yd³
C. 1588.9 yd³
D. 1906.6 yd³

6.G.2

2. There is a prism that is 5 3/4 cm wide. It has a width of 11 cm and a depth of 8 1/2 cm. What is its volume? (Round to tenths.)

A. 517.8 cm³
B. 526.5 cm³
C. 537.6 cm³
D. 540.3 cm³

6.G.2

3. The rectangular prisms below are made of unit cubes that have 1/2-inch sides. What is the volume of the prism?

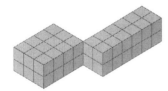

A. 4 in³
B. 6 in³
C. 8 in³
D. 12 in³

6.G.2

4. There are 3 complete layers in the picture below. If each unit cube is 1/4 - yard, what is the volume of the shape?

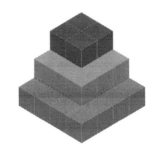

A. $\frac{1}{4}$ yds³
B. $\frac{7}{16}$ yds³
C. $\frac{15}{32}$ yds³
D. $\frac{29}{64}$ yds³

6.G.2

5. Which equation is represented in the data from the chart below?

x	y
5	2
10	4
15	6

A. $x = 0.4y$
B. $y = 0.4x$
C. $y = \frac{1}{4}x$
D. $x = \frac{1}{4}y$

6.EE.9

6. What is the least common multiple of 10 and 8?

A. 10
B. 20
C. 40
D. 60

6.NS.4

DAY 6
CHALLENGE QUESTION

If there were FOUR of the rectangular prisms from #1, what would be their total volume?

6.G.2

Congratulations! You've made it to Week 20! This week you will study polygons on a coordinate plane to find lengths and answer real-world questions. You will also see nets that are a two-dimensional picture of a three-dimensional object. Finish strong!

You can find detailed video explanations to each problem in the book by visiting:
ArgoPrep.com

WEEK 20 · DAY I

ARGOPREP.COM

Use the figures below to answer questions 1 – 4.

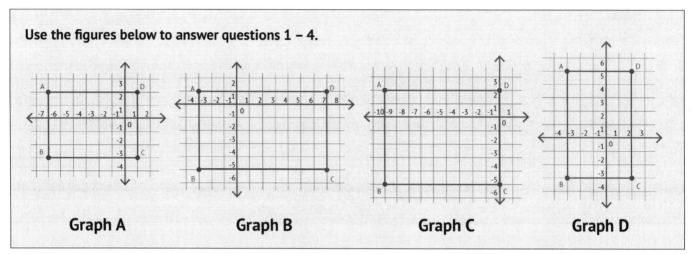

| Graph A | Graph B | Graph C | Graph D |

1. Which graph above shows a rectangle with the coordinates below?

A (-9, 2) B (-9, -5) C (0, -5) D (0, 2)

A. Graph A
B. Graph B
C. Graph C
D. Graph D

6.G.3

2. Which graph above shows a rectangle with the coordinates below?

A (-3, 1) B (-3, -5) C (7, -5) D (7, 1)

A. Graph A
B. Graph B
C. Graph C
D. Graph D

6.G.3

3. Which graph above shows a rectangle with the coordinates below?

A (-3, 5) B (-3, -3) C (2, -3) D (2, 5)

A. Graph A
B. Graph B
C. Graph C
D. Graph D

6.G.3

4. Which graph above shows a rectangle with the coordinates below?

A (-6, 2) B (-6, -3) C (1, -3) D (1, 2)

A. Graph A
B. Graph B
C. Graph C
D. Graph D

6.G.3

On a rectangular coordinate system, always begin at the origin (0, 0).

Michael lives at the origin on the coordinate system below. Here are the locations of some building he might travel to: (A) school, (B) store, (C) gym, (D) car wash, (E) library and (F) police. **Use the graph to answer questions 1 – 4.**

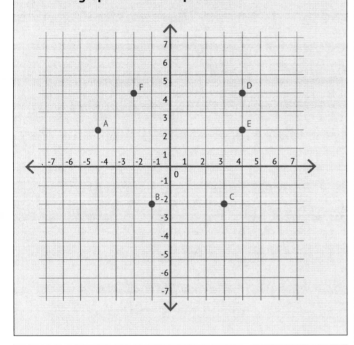

1. Michael wants to go the library. What route can he take from his house to get to the library?

   A. Go 4 units right and then 2 units up
   B. Go 4 units up and then 2 units right
   C. Go 4 units up and then 2 units left
   D. Go 4 units left and then 2 units up

6.G.3

2. After the library, Michael needs to go see his dad who is a police officer. What route can Michael take from the library?

   A. Go 6 units left and then 2 units down
   B. Go 2 units up and then 6 units left
   C. Go 5 units left and then 2 units up
   D. Go 2 units up and then 5 units left

6.G.3

3. From the police station Michael travels 4 units down, then 1 unit right and 2 units down. Where has Michael gone?

   A. car wash
   B. gym
   C. school
   D. store

6.G.3

4. Michael returns home. Tomorrow he will need to go to school. What route can he take to get to school?

   A. Go 2 units down and then 3 units right
   B. Go 2 units up and then 4 units right
   C. Go 4 units up and then 4 units right
   D. Go 2 units up and then 4 units left

6.G.3

GPS works off of a grid-like system. You can use a coordinate system to determine direction.

The figure below is measured in centimeters. **Use the figure to answer questions 1 – 2.**

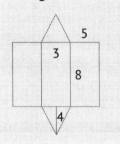

The figure below is measured in feet. **Use the figure to answer questions 4 – 6.**

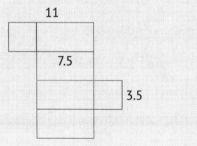

1. Which three-dimensional shape is formed by the figure above?

    A. rectangular prism
    B. triangular prism
    C. pyramid
    D. cube

6.G.4

4. Which three-dimensional shape is formed by the figure above?

    A. rectangular prism
    B. triangular prism
    C. pyramid
    D. cube

6.G.4

2. If Naomi were to wrap the figure above, how much paper would she need?

    A. 76 cm²   **C.** 98 cm²
    B. 88 cm²   **D.** 116 cm²

6.G.4

5. What is the volume of the figure above?

    A. 91.875 ft³   **C.** 201.5 ft³
    B. 118.125 ft³   **D.** 288.75 ft³

6.G.2

3. What is the greatest common factor of 37 and 41?

    A. 1   **C.** 7
    B. 3   **D.** 11

6.NS.4

6. If this figure were covered with wood, how much wood would be needed?

    A. 77.0 ft²   **C.** 129.5 ft²
    B. 99.5 ft²   **D.** 154.0 ft²

6.G.4

A net is formed when a three-dimensional object is "unfolded" and laid flat.

Use the figure below is measured in meters. Use the drawing to answer questions 1 – 2.

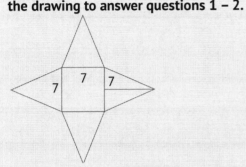

7 7 7

Use the drawing below to answer questions 3 – 5.

5 inches

5 inches

5 inches

1. Which three-dimensional shape is formed by the figure above?

  A. rectangular prism
  B. triangular prism
  C. pyramid
  D. cube

6.G.4

2. Olivia was making a gift box in the shape shown above. How much cardboard would Olivia need to make the box?

  A. 73.5 m²
  B. 147 m²
  C. 198.5 m²
  D. 245.0 m²

6.G.4

3. Which three-dimensional shape is formed by the figure above?

  A. rectangular prism
  B. triangular prism
  C. pyramid
  D. cube

6.G.4

4. What is the volume of the figure above?

  A. 75 in³   **C.** 125 in³
  B. 100 in³   **D.** 150 in³

6.G.2

5. What is the surface area of the figure above?

  A. 75 in²   **C.** 125 in²
  B. 100 in²   **D.** 150 in²

6.G.4

When looking at a net, consider how the shape might "fold" at the "joints" of the two-dimensional shape.

Use the figure below to answer questions 1 – 5.

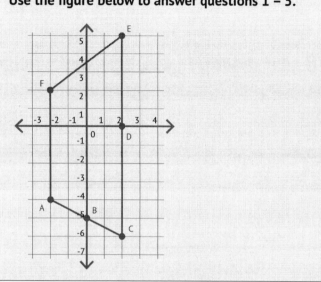

1. Which 2 segments have the same length?

A. *AC* and *EF*   C. *AB* and *EF*
B. *CD* and *AF*   D. *DE* and *DC* 6.G.3

2. What is the area of the figure above?

A. 25 units²   C. 36 units²
B. 34 units²   D. 68 units² 6.G.3

3. What is the distance between Points E and C?

A. 9 units   C. 11 units
B. 10 units   D. 12 units 6.NS.8

4. How many units is Point C from (-7,-6)?

A. 9 units
B. 10 units
C. 11 units
D. 12 units

6.NS.8

5. If the figure were 6 units tall, what would be its volume?

A. 150 units³
B. 204 units³
C. 216 units³
D. 408 units³

6.G.2

6. The vertices for a quadrilateral are given below. What is the distance between Points A and D?

A (-2,-4), B (0,-7), C (5, 3), D (-2, 5)

A. 0
B. 1
C. 5
D. 9

6.G.3

DAY 6

CHALLENGE QUESTION

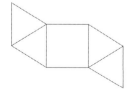

What three-dimensional shape has a net like the one shown to the left?

6.G.3

THE END!

Assessment

ARGOPREP.COM

VIDEO
EXPLANATIONS

Great job finishing all 20 weeks!
You should be ready for any test.
Try this assessment to see how
much you've learned - good luck!

ASSESSMENT

1. The coordinates of the vertices of a rectangle are A (-5, 1), B (3, 1), C (3, -4) and D (-5, -4). What are the dimensions of the rectangle?

    A. 2 units by 5 units
    B. 3 units by 4 units
    C. 4 units by 8 units
    D. 5 units by 8 units

6.NS.8

Rhea kept track of her dog's weight and the results are shown below. **Use this information to answer questions 3 – 4.** Round your answer to the nearest hundredth.

Weight (in pounds):	34	38	37	37	41	46	39

Steve's bank balance for 5 days was recorded and is shown below. **Use this information to answer question 2.**

Day	Balance ($)
1	– 299
2	146
3	– 297
4	– 71
5	312

3. What is the range of the data?

    A. 5
    B. 8
    C. 9
    D. 12

6.SP.2

2. Steve wants to plot the balances on a number line. Which day will be the furthest to the left on the number line?

    A. 1
    B. 2
    C. 3
    D. 4

6.NS.7

4. What is the mean of the data?

    A. 37.6
    B. 38.9
    C. 39.4
    D. 40.1

6.SP.2

5. Which expression is equivalent to

7 (10 – 2)?

A. 710 – 72
B. 70 – 2
C. 70 – 14
D. 68

6.NS.4

6. Shelly owed $55.71. Which action will allow Shelly to become debt-free?

A. Shelly can borrow $55.71 from her friend.
B. Shelly can pay $32 on her loan.
C. Shelly can spend $55.71.
D. Shelly can pay $55.71 on her loan.

6.NS.5

7. The rectangular prism below is made of cubes that have 1/2-inch sides. What is the volume of the prism?

A. $2\frac{5}{6}$ in³

B. $8\frac{1}{2}$ in³

C. $15\frac{3}{4}$ in³

D. $21\frac{7}{8}$ in³

6.G.2

Use the coordinate system below to answer questions 8 – 9.

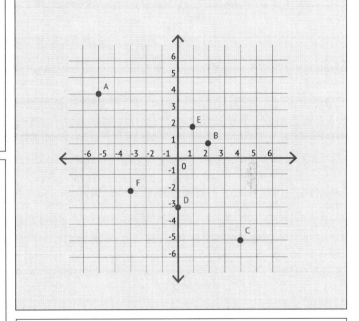

8. What is the y-coordinate of Point C?

A. – 4
B. – 5
C. 4
D. 5

6.NS.6

9. What point is located at (1, 2)?

A. A
B. C
C. D
D. E

6.NS.6

ASSESSMENT

10. The corn cost 4 dollars less than the broccoli. If the broccoli cost b, how much did the corn cost?

A. $b - 4$ **C.** $b + 4$

B. $4 - b$ **D.** $\frac{1}{4} b$

6.EE.6

Lana recorded how many kilometers she ran in a day. Her records are shown below. **Use the information to answer questions 11 – 12.**

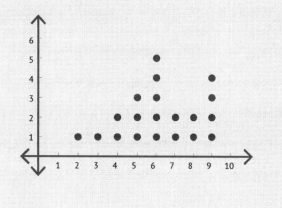

11. What is the farthest distance Lana traveled on 1 day?

A. 5 km
B. 6 km
C. 8 km
D. 9 km

6.SP.5

12. How many days did Lana record her running?

A. 15
B. 18
C. 20
D. 22

6.SP.5

13. What is the value of the expression below?

$$2^3 + \frac{1}{4}(8^2 + 12^1)$$

A. 15
B. 27
C. 46
D. 108

6.EE.1

14. How many cups of mashed potatoes would 4 people get if they equally shared 3/4 cup of potatoes?

A. $\frac{1}{3}$ cup

B. $\frac{1}{4}$ cup

C. $\frac{3}{4}$ cup

D. $\frac{3}{16}$ cup

6.NS.1

15. The PE department had 356 dodge balls that needed to be put in storage. If each box could hold 15 dodge balls, how many boxes would they need?

A. 22
B. 23
C. 24
D. 25

6.NS.2

18. What is the value of $\frac{7}{12} \div \frac{8}{15}$?

A. $\frac{16}{45}$

B. $\frac{32}{35}$

C. $\frac{45}{16}$

D. $\frac{35}{32}$

6.NS.1

16. What is the value of the expression below when $m = -6$ and $n = 3$?

$\frac{m}{n} - 8m + n$

A. -47
B. -44
C. 49
D. 53

6.EE.2

19. Which question below is a statistical question?

A. How many moons does Jupiter have?
B. What is the largest star?
C. Do you like pizza?
D. How long can 6th graders hold their breath?

6.SP.1

17. Twenty-five days of weather were recorded. It was found that there were 12 sunny days, 8 cloudy days and the rest were rainy. What is the ratio of rainy days to total days?

A. 1:4
B. 1:5
C. 4:1
D. 5:1

6.RP.1

20. Fifty-four folding chairs cost $1188. What was the cost of 1 chair?

A. $18
B. $20
C. $22
D. $24

6.RP.2

21. What is the solution to this equation:

$\frac{2}{5}w = 12\frac{3}{5}$?

A. $w = 30\frac{1}{2}$

B. $w = 30\frac{4}{5}$

C. $w = 31\frac{1}{2}$

D. $w = 31\frac{4}{5}$

6.EE.7

22. Shana had 356 points during the season. If she played in 20 games, how many points did she average per game? Round your answer to the nearest tenth.

A. 16.8
B. 17.8
C. 19.2
D. 19.6

6.NS.3

23. Which three-dimensional shape is formed by the figure?

A. rectangular prism
B. triangular prism
C. pyramid
D. cube

6.G.4

24. What is the surface area of the figure?

A. 298.5 m²
B. 375.0 m²
C. 412.5 m²
D. 489.0 m²

6.G.4

Below is a two-dimensional net for a three-dimensional figure. **Use the drawing to answer questions 23 – 24.**

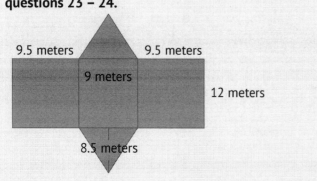

9.5 meters   9.5 meters
9 meters
12 meters
8.5 meters

25. Which two expressions are equivalent for any value of q?

A. $15q + 12$ and $3(5q + 4)$
B. $2q + 8$ and $q(q + 8)$
C. $q(7 - 8)$ and $7q - 8$
D. $4q(q - 1)$ and $4q - 4$

6.EE.4

26. Which equation has the solution

$d = -3$?

   A. $15 - d = 12$
   B. $2d + 3 = -3$
   C. $-5d = -15$
   D. $d = 10 - 13 + 1$

6.EE.5

27. The Hoosiers need to get no more than 78 penalty points to go on to the playoffs. Which inequality shows how many penalty points, p, the Hoosiers can get and still make the playoffs?

   A. $p > 78$
   B. $p < 78$
   C. $p \geq 78$
   D. $p \leq 78$

6.EE.8

28. What is another way to write:

$6(4g - h)$?

6.EE.3

29. What is the greatest common factor of 40 and 50?

6.NS.4

30. 25.6 is what percent of 32?

6.RP.3

31. The hexagon below is made of 6 triangles that each have a base of 4 inches and a height of 5 inches. What is the area of the hexagon?

6.G.1

32. What is another way to write:

$u + u + u + u + u + u$

as a single term?

6.EE.3

33. What is 120% of 315?

6.RP.3

34. What is the least common multiple of 12 and 6?

6.NS.4

35. Tomas bought 16 birthday cards for $28. Write an equation to show the relationship between the number of birthday cards, *s*, and *C*, the total cost for the cards.

6.EE.9

Use the drawing below to answer questions 36 – 37.

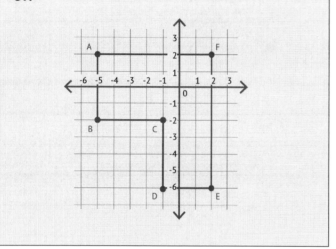

36. Which 3 sides have the same length?

6.G.3

37. What is the perimeter of the figure?

6.G.3

Below are four different data sets. **Use the sets below to answer question 38.**

Table A

2	7	4	2
4	3	5	6
5	4	6	5

Table B

7	5	2	4
4	6	4	5
5	3	5	6

Table C

5	2	6	4
3	4	4	2
2	5	1	6

Table D

5	2	4	2
5	7	6	8
2	3	8	5

38. Which data set is graphed below?

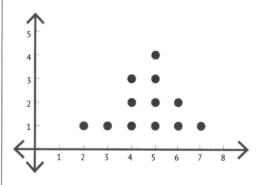

6.SP.4

Javier measured sunflowers. **The results are below. Use this data to answer questions 39 – 40.**

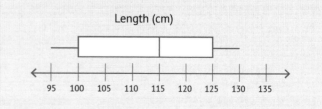

39. What is the median for the data set shown?

6.SP.3

40. What is the range for the data set shown?

6.SP.3

41. What is the value of the expression below?

$8 + 12^2 \times 3$

6.EE.1

42. Maria mowed the lawn for m minutes, which was 13 minutes longer than Manuel worked in the garden. Write an algebraic expression to show how long Manuel worked in the garden. less points than the Indians. How many points did the Indians score?

6.EE.6

43. What is the value of the expression $9r - 5s + 3^3$ if $r = 2/3$ and $s = -2$?

6.EE.2

44. What is the solution to this equation:

$4a = -10$?

6.EE.7

ANSWER KEYS

ARGOPREP.COM

VIDEO
EXPLANATIONS

ANSWER KEYS

WEEK 1

DAY 1	DAY 2	DAY 3	DAY 4	DAY 5
1: D	**1:** B	**1:** A	**1:** B	**1:** B
2: A	**2:** C	**2:** B	**2:** D	**2:** C
3: B	**3:** A	**3:** B	**3:** B	**3:** B
4: D	**4:** D	**4:** D	**4:** A	**4:** A
5: A	**5:** D	**5:** B	**5:** C	**5:** C
6: D	**6:** A	**6:** D	**6:** C	**6:** D

WEEK 2

DAY 1	DAY 2	DAY 3	DAY 4	DAY 5
1: B	**1:** A	**1:** B	**1:** D	**1:** D
2: A	**2:** C	**2:** D	**2:** B	**2:** C
3: C	**3:** A	**3:** B	**3:** B	**3:** B
4: D	**4:** B	**4:** A	**4:** C	**4:** A
5: B	**5:** A	**5:** D	**5:** C	**5:** A
6: D	**6:** D	**6:** A		**6:** B

WEEK 3

DAY 1	DAY 2	DAY 3	DAY 4	DAY 5
1: D	**1:** C	**1:** B	**1:** B	**1:** A
2: C	**2:** A	**2:** D	**2:** C	**2:** C
3: D	**3:** C	**3:** C	**3:** C	**3:** B
4: D	**4:** C	**4:** B	**4:** D	**4:** B
5: C	**5:** D	**5:** B	**5:** D	**5:** D
	6: C	**6:** B	**6:** C	**6:** A

WEEK 4

DAY 1	DAY 2	DAY 3	DAY 4	DAY 5
1: C	**1:** B	**1:** C	**1:** D	**1:** D
2: B	**2:** C	**2:** D	**2:** B	**2:** A
3: A	**3:** B	**3:** D	**3:** C	**3:** A
4: D	**4:** A	**4:** D	**4:** B	**4:** B
5: B	**5:** C	**5:** B	**5:** B	**5:** C
6: C	**6:** D		**6:** C	**6:** C

WEEK 5

DAY 1	DAY 2	DAY 3	DAY 4	DAY 5
1: A	**1:** D	**1:** C	**1:** D	**1:** D
2: C	**2:** C	**2:** B	**2:** A	**2:** C
3: B	**3:** B	**3:** D	**3:** B	**3:** C
4: B	**4:** D	**4:** C	**4:** A	**4:** C
	5: C	**5:** A	**5:** C	**5:** B
	6: D	**6:** C	**6:** D	**6:** D

WEEK 6

DAY 1	DAY 2	DAY 3	DAY 4	DAY 5
1: D	**1:** D	**1:** B	**1:** C	**1:** C
2: C	**2:** A	**2:** D	**2:** B	**2:** B
3: A	**3:** D	**3:** A	**3:** A	**3:** C
4: B	**4:** B	**4:** B	**4:** D	**4:** A
5: B	**5:** C	**5:** A	**5:** A	**5:** A
6: A	**6:** D		**6:** A	**6:** D

WEEK 7

DAY 1	DAY 2	DAY 3	DAY 4	DAY 5
1: A	**1:** D	**1:** B	**1:** A	**1:** A
2: C	**2:** C	**2:** D	**2:** B	**2:** B
3: C	**3:** C	**3:** D	**3:** C	**3:** C
4: B	**4:** B	**4:** B	**4:** A	**4:** A
5: D	**5:** C	**5:** A	**5:** D	**5:** A
6: C	**6:** A	**6:** D	**6:** D	**6:** C

WEEK 8

DAY 1	DAY 2	DAY 3	DAY 4	DAY 5
1: A	**1:** D	**1:** A	**1:** D	**1:** C
2: B	**2:** B	**2:** D	**2:** B	**2:** D
3: A	**3:** C	**3:** C	**3:** A	**3:** A
4: C	**4:** C	**4:** A	**4:** C	**4:** C
5: C	**5:** A	**5:** B	**5:** B	**5:** C
6: D	**6:** D	**6:** B	**6:** C	**6:** D

WEEK 9

DAY 1	DAY 2	DAY 3	DAY 4	DAY 5
1: B	1: A	1: D	1: A	1: A
2: C	2: A	2: B	2: B	2: D
3: B	3: D	3: C	3: C	3: B
4: A	4: B	4: B	4: C	4: A
5: C	5: C	5: B	5: A	5: D
6: B	6: B	6: C	6: C	6: D

WEEK 10

DAY 1	DAY 2	DAY 3	DAY 4	DAY 5
1: B	1: A	1: B	1: D	1: C
2: B	2: C	2: C	2: A	2: B
3: D	3: B	3: C	3: D	3: D
4: C	4: A	4: D	4: B	4: C
5: A	5: C	5: C	5: A	5: D
6: B	6: D	6: A	6: B	6: A

WEEK 11

DAY 1	DAY 2	DAY 3	DAY 4	DAY 5
1: A	1: C	1: D	1: D	1: B
2: B	2: C	2: C	2: D	2: B
3: D	3: D	3: A	3: A	3: D
4: A	4: C	4: D	4: B	4: A
5: C	5: B	5: B	5: B	5: B
	6: A			

WEEK 12

DAY 1	DAY 2	DAY 3	DAY 4	DAY 5
1: B	1: B	1: C	1: A	1: D
2: A	2: D	2: B	2: B	2: C
3: C	3: A	3: C	3: B	3: B
4: D	4: D	4: D	4: A	4: B
5: C	5: B	5: B	5: C	5: A
6: B	6: D			

WEEK 13

DAY 1	DAY 2	DAY 3	DAY 4	DAY 5
1: C	1: B	1: A	1: B	1: D
2: B	2: C	2: C	2: C	2: B
3: C	3: B	3: B	3: C	3: A
4: D	4: D	4: B	4: A	4: C
5: B	5: A	5: A	5: D	5: B
6: A	6: D		6: B	6: D

WEEK 14

DAY 1	DAY 2	DAY 3	DAY 4	DAY 5
1: D	1: A	1: C	1: C	1: D
2: B	2: D	2: B	2: B	2: B
3: C	3: B	3: C	3: A	3: B
4: D	4: C	4: B	4: C	4: B
5: C	5: C	5: A	5: A	5: C
6: C				

WEEK 15

DAY 1	DAY 2	DAY 3	DAY 4	DAY 5
1: C	1: B	1: B	1: C	1: D
2: D	2: C	2: C	2: C	2: B
3: C	3: D	3: A	3: B	3: C
4: B	4: A	4: C	4: A	4: D
5: C	5: A	5: C	5: C	5: C
6: D	6: B	6: C		6: C

WEEK 16

DAY 1	DAY 2	DAY 3	DAY 4	DAY 5
1: A	1: D	1: B	1: A	1: C
2: C	2: A	2: C	2: C	2: A
3: D	3: B	3: D	3: D	3: B
4: B	4: C	4: A	4: B	4: D
5: D	5: B	5: A	5: C	5: B

ANSWER KEY

WEEK 17

DAY 1	DAY 2	DAY 3	DAY 4	DAY 5
1: C	1: D	1: B	1: A	1: C
2: A	2: A	2: D	2: D	2: A
3: A	3: C	3: A	3: C	3: D
4: D	4: B	4: D	4: B	4: B
5: C	5: D	5: C	5: B	5: C
6: C	6: B	6: B	6: A	6: B

WEEK 18

DAY 1	DAY 2	DAY 3	DAY 4	DAY 5
1: C	1: C	1: B	1: B	1: D
2: A	2: B	2: B	2: D	2: C
3: C	3: C	3: D	3: C	3: B
4: B	4: B	4: D	4: B	4: B
5: A	5: B	5: D	5: C	5: A
6: C	6: A	6: D	6: B	6: D

WEEK 19

DAY 1	DAY 2	DAY 3	DAY 4	DAY 5
1: D	1: C	1: A	1: A	1: D
2: A	2: C	2: B	2: B	2: C
3: B	3: A	3: D	3: B	3: B
4: D	4: D	4: C	4: D	4: D
5: A	5: B	5: A	5: C	5: B
6: B	6: B	6: D	6: B	6: C

WEEK 20

DAY 1	DAY 2	DAY 3	DAY 4	DAY 5
1: C	1: A	1: B	1: C	1: B
2: B	2: B	2: D	2: B	2: B
3: D	3: D	3: A	3: D	3: C
4: A	4: D	4: A	4: C	4: A
		5: A	5: D	5: B
		6: C		6: D

Challenge Question

Week 1: 3 3/4 cups
Week 2: 59 inches
Week 3: 661 yards
Week 4: Quadrant I
Week 5: – 15
Week 6: 18x - 28.5y + 12
Week 7: $5a + 2b - 34$
Week 8: C – 5
Week 9: Length: $12b$ cm
Perimeter: $48b$ cm
Week 10: x < - 1/2
Week 11: 12
Week 12: 325 miles
Week 13: Any question that samples more than 1 person/thing and has a range of possible answers is a statistical question.
Week 14: 48.4

Week 15: 12
Week 16:
Week 17: 75

Week 18: 58.5 m²
Week 19: 7626.5 yd³
Week 20: pyramid

Assessment

1: D	15: C	28: $24g - 6h$
2: A	16: C	29: 10
D: D	17: B	30: 80%
4: B	18: D	31: 60 in²
5: C	19: D	32: $6u$
6: D	20: C	33: 378
7: D	21: C	34: 12
8: B	22: B	35: $C = 1.75s$
9: D	23: B	36: AB, BC and CD
10: A	24: C	37: 30 units
11: D	25: A	38: Table B
12: C	26: B	39: 115
13: B	27: D	40: 35
14: D		41: 440
		42: $m - 13$
		43: 43
		44: $a = 2.5$

Made in the USA
Middletown, DE
15 September 2018